Contemporary Mexican Drama
in Translation

Volume I: Azcárate, Rascón,
Urtusástegui

Introduction and translations
by Myra S. Gann

Danzón Press
14 Hamilton St.
Potsdam, N.Y. 13676

© Myra S. Gann, 1994

ISBN 0-9643288-0-1

CONTENTS

INTRODUCTION

"As strange as it may seem, the decade of the crisis has been the decade of the boom in Mexican dramaturgy" ["Por extraño que parezca, la década de la crisis ha sido la del auge de la dramaturgia mexicana"]. Thus began an article published in *Semanal*, the weekly cultural supplement of the daily *La Jornada*, in the last issue of the decade (José Ramón Enríquez, "La dramaturgia mexicana en su auge de crisis," #28, Dec. 24, 1989, pp. 20-25).

During the seventies it was commonly accepted that plays written by living Mexicans, unless Emilio Carballido were the author, would be seen only in very experimental theaters, produced by marginal groups who dared take a great risk, since theatergoers (supposedly) consistently preferred contemporary American and European, or classical anything, to national drama. But the eighties were different. During this decade Víctor Hugo Rascón Banda and Oscar Liera had at least one major production every year, while Jesús González Dávila and Vicente Leñero were staged seven times. And Tomás Urtusástegui, who before 1980 had never written a play, had his first professional performance in 1982 and saw a new play produced every year until 1989, when in different parts of the country, in amateur and professional contexts combined, there were over sixty different productions of his plays. The number of dramatic composition workshops multiplied, launching many new playwrights, including, for the first time, an increasing number of women. And, of course, Emilio Carballido continued to supply theater companies with outstanding works, approximately one every other year, his comedy *Rosa de dos aromas* setting the national record for the longest single run of any play. The general feeling among playwrights was that the tides had changed, that directors and producers were actually hungry for new Mexican plays, that they were being preferred over imports, and that there was an unprecedented interest in examining Mexican reality, however painful that examination might be.

How can this remarkable change in popularity of the playwrights and in attitude of the theatergoers be accounted for? Some believe that

the economic crisis itself was responsible, as Rascón Banda foresaw as
early as 1982:

> . . . maybe, faced with the impossibility of producing refried
> versions of North American or English plays, we will begin to
> draw on our national raw material; maybe, faced with the
> difficulty of obtaining funds to import second-class movies and
> third-class television programs, we will turn to the native-born
> to write, direct, act and produce. It could be that, faced with the
> lack of economic resources for productions of one, two and
> three million pesos, to which some privileged persons have
> become accustomed, we will have to rely on ingenuity, talent
> and creativity to substitute for devalued pesos. It may very
> well be. . .
> [. . .pudiera suceder que, ante la imposibilidad de producir
> refritos teatrales de Norteamérica e Inglaterra, se acuda a la
> materia prima nacional; pudiera ocurrir que, ante la dificultad
> de conseguir divisas para importar cine de segunda y televisión
> de tercera, se recurra a los nativos para escribir, dirigir, actuar y
> producir. Pudiera ser que, ante la falta de recursos económicos
> para las producciones de uno, dos y tres millones de pesos, a
> que tan mal se acostumbraron algunos privilegiados, se tenga
> que acudir al ingenio, al talento y a la creatividad, para suplir la
> carencia de los devaluados pesos. Bien pudiera ser. . .]
> ("Nueva dramaturgia mexicana," *Latin American Theatre
> Review*, 18/2, spring 1985, p. 92.)

If Mexico was to have any theater at all during those years, Rascón
believed, it was to be Mexican theater, the only affordable one. In
addition, playwrights seeing opportunities opening up began to tailor
their works to the crisis situation, making them even more appealing: a
large percentage of the plays written during this period have a very small
cast of characters and can be performed in black box theaters with few
or no props.   These dramatists often joke that they have found the true
meaning of Jerzy Grotowski's "poor theater."

It must also be remarked that the efforts of Emilio Carballido, Hugo
Argüelles and Vicente Leñero seemed to finally reach fruition in the
eighties. These more established playwrights devoted a substantial
amount of their time over the years, in Carballido's case ever since the
late sixties, to the formation of the current generation of playwrights, the
"New Dramatists" and the "New New Dramatists" as well. It is to
Carballido's decade-long writing workshop held at the Polytechnic
Institute and his subsequent constant mentoring of young writers, along
with Arguelles' and Leñero's workshops of the late seventies and entire

eighties, that most of the plays which reached the stage during the "boom" of the eighties can be attributed.

The four playwrights selected for this volume were active participants in the Leñero workshop, Vicente Leñero always insisting that he was not a "teacher" but, rather, an organizing force behind the workshop, a participant in the same way as the others. The plays themselves, Leñero's in particular, reflect the interest of this group in returning the dramatic text to its rightful place in the theater--first place-- and, similarly, in experimenting with new realisms, with the intention of expressing more faithfully the disjointed, non-teleological view of reality of the eighties.

After years of seeing the text used as a "pretext" for the theatrical event, the Leñero playwrights called for a renewed respect for the written word and for authors to have a place at least equal to that of the director in the making of the final product (see Azcárate et al, "Textos y pretextos del teatro mexicano: once dramaturgos debaten sobre los textos, los pretextos, los montajes y las rutas del teatro mexicano," in *Semanal*, #24, Nov. 26, 1989, pp. 26-33). They saw themselves as distinct from playwrights of previous "text-centered" movements who considered themselves "men of letters" rather than "men of the theater" and for whom publication of the play was as satisfactory as a production of it. These dramatists of the eighties were writing with the stage and its audience in mind at all times, production being their primary goal, even though they chose to give priority to the word (and what it *does*) over actions (and what they *say*) (see Leñero's article "Dramaturgia para hoy o para nunca" in *Proceso* 755, April 22, 1991, pp. 48-49).

The return to realism was a direct result of the renewed emphasis on the text, and led to Rascón's poetic realism, Leñero's hyperrealism, Azcárate's comic realism and Urtusástegui's combination of farce with realistic comedy. The realities depicted in these plays are very specifically Mexican, without falling into the *costumbrismo* of previous generations, which frequently created light-hearted descriptions of local color, mostly rural. The situations are fictitious, but the language and the motivations of the characters are extremely true to life; in the case of Leñero's *No One Knows Anything*, one of the characters was so recognizable as a Mexican dignitary that the play was closed down until the author made a few minor changes to make his character less reminiscent of the real-life model.

The four plays are quite representative of the overall national production of the eighties, especially with regard to theme; in them, as in a large number of works not included here, hypocrisy--with the corruption, deception and double standards that stem from it--is seen as the underlying cause of most of the problems facing Mexico today.

We can only conclude that Mexican drama of the eighties reflects the profound desire for change that can be felt in most areas of Mexican society today. But fortunately for us, these plays follow the classical Spanish norm of combining *enseñanza* ("teaching") with *deleite* ("pleasure"); they are as pleasurable to read as they are informative about contemporary Mexican society.

Groups or individuals interested in obtaining permission to perform the plays can make contact with the playwrights through me.

--Myra S. Gann
--State University of New York at Potsdam

Leonor Azcárate (Mexico City, 1955), is the youngest of the playwrights included in this volume, and the only woman. She represents a growing number of women who have begun to write for the Mexican stage since the late seventies, her friend Sabina Berman being the most prolific and well-known of this group. (Both Azcárate and Berman were active members of the Leñero workshop mentioned in my introduction.) She writes both comic and serious plays, including radio drama and children's plays; she is probably most well known for the two plays she saw staged professionally last year: *Pasajero de medianoche (Midnight Passenger)*, a musical aimed at educating teenagers about AIDS, and *Trabajo sucio (Dirty Work)*, a play about torture and rape.

In 1988 *Margarita Came Back to Life (Margarita resucitó)* won Honorable Mention in the annual play writing contest held by the Sociedad General de Escritores Mexicanos, but to date it remains unpublished and unperformed, due to what appears to be a series of strokes of bad luck on the part of well-meaning directors and publishers. It is a delightful piece of satirical criticism of Mexican middle class family life, which promotes the dependence and selfishness of children to the point where the mother is a "non-entity," a person seen as someone to fulfill the needs of others, with no desire of her own, no needs, no role in the world beyond the family unit. Though much of the action is farcical, the dialogue is very realistic, the humor deriving in great part from the cleverness of the author at recreating the ingenious insults and retorts so common among Mexican middle class youths. All of Leonor Azcárate's work underscores the less than satisfactory position and treatment of women in Mexico; *Margarita. . .* is her only comedy that does so, and is, in my opinion, her most effective play. We will be hearing increasingly more from and about this playwright; and hopefully we will see *Margarita Came Back to Life* brought to the stage in both Mexico and the United States.

MARGARITA CAME BACK TO LIFE

by Leonor Azcárate

CHARACTERS:

Mama Rita, 54 years old
Gonzalo, 33 years old
Kiqui, 31 years old
Silvia, 29 years old
Alberto, 18 years old
Granny-Granma, 70 years old

SET:

Living room-dining room. There is a stairway to the upstairs rooms.
At stage rear there is a door which leads to the kitchen and at the other
end a door to the outside. Also, at the rear is a window which looks on
to the street. In the living room there is living room furniture suitable
for eight people, including a coffee table, a stereo set, a bookcase, a bar,
a television set and a VCR. The dining room consists of a table with
eight chairs. The style is typical middle class.

*   *   *

>*Gonzalo is reading the newspaper and Mama Rita is knitting a scarf. They are seated face to face in comfortable living room armchairs.*

GONZALO: *(Sneezes)*
MAMA RITA: Bless you, dear.
GONZALO: *(Sneezes again)*
MAMA RITA: Bless you, honey.
GONZALO: *(Sneezes again)*
MAMA RITA: Gonzalito, I think you're getting a cold!
GONZALO: It's your cabbage dinner.
MAMA RITA: What an idea, baby. Put on a sweater.
GONZALO: The same thing always happens to me.
MAMA RITA: No, you're just a little under the weather.
GONZALO: I'm talking about your cabbage dinner.
MAMA RITA: Yes, yes, I know what you're going to say.
GONZALO: No you don't.
MAMA RITA: Yes, I do. You're going to say that a psychoanalyst told you that everything I do irritates your nasal membranes.
GONZALO: *(Laughing halfheartedly)* I told you so.
MAMA RITA: Told me what?
GONZALO: *(Sneezes)*
MAMA RITA: Bless you!
GONZALO: Thanks. *(He sneezes again)*

>*Silence.*

MAMA RITA: That's right, mothers are awful.
GONZALO: You love to exaggerate.
MAMA RITA: *(Makes a face)* Mh. . .
GONZALO: Kiqui's favorite dish was always cabbage dinner.
MAMA RITA: It still is, but I know what you're getting at. I know all of you very well.
GONZALO: Mama, don't start.
MAMA RITA: Right now I should be with my friends.
GONZALO: What about me? I missed my Proctologists' conference because of your dinner.
MAMA RITA: It's not my dinner. I didn't force you to come.

GONZALO: I hate cabbage dinner.

MAMA RITA: Leave your sister alone, Gonzalo.

> *Alberto comes down the stairway,*
> *enters and goes to the stereo. He turns*
> *it on immediately. We hear the music*
> *of Tina Turner at top volume. Gonzalo*
> *and Mama Rita keep talking, though*
> *we can't make out what they're saying.*
> *Meanwhile, Alberto lip sincs the song,*
> *addressing himself to one of the*
> *speakers of the stereo system.*

GONZALO: You should have made it clear that this dinner party is for Kiqui.

MAMA RITA: Nothing I do matters to you all.

GONZALO: We're all going to eat, not just Kiqui.

MAMA RITA: Put on a sweater and shut up.

GONZALO: *(To Alberto)* Turn it down!

MAMA RITA: I'd like to know what you all ever do for me.

GONZALO: *(Sneezes)*

MAMA RITA: *(To Alberto)* Sweetheart, turn it down.

> *Alberto disgruntledly turns the music off.*

MAMA RITA: *(To Alberto)* Honey, be a little considerate of Granny-Granma.

ALBERTO: *(He goes to sit down in one of the armchairs.)* You can't do anything around here. It's just like a prison.

MAMA RITA: Granny-Granma just got here and I'm sure she'll want to sleep. Be fair, let her rest.

ALBERTO: I already turned it off, Mama.

GONZALO: *(Sneezes)*

MAMA RITA AND ALBERTO: Bless you!

> *Granny-Granma appears from upstairs,*
> *leaning on the banister of the stairway.*

GRAN: Rita. . . Rita. . . help me down. . . Rita. . .

GONZALO: She's up.

MAMA RITA: Leave her there.

GRAN: Help me down. . . Rita. . .

MAMA RITA: Don't pay any attention to her. Maybe she'll go to sleep.

GRAN: Rita. . . help me down. . . Rita. . .

MAMA RITA: What is it, Mama?

GRAN: Help me down.

MAMA RITA: Your turn to help her, Alberto.

> *Alberto, in a bad mood, gets up and goes up the stairs.   While Alberto and Granny-Granma come down, Gonzalo reads the newspaper and Mama Rita knits a scarf. Granny-Granma whines a little with each step.   When they reach the living room, Granny-Granma sits next to Mama Rita.*

GRAN: *(To Alberto)* Thanks, sweetie, you're the light of my life. *(She smiles as if talking to an absent audience.)* Gonzalito, how handsome you look.

> *Gonzalo, his face hidden behind the newspaper, sneezes.*

MAMA RITA: Mama, why don't you try to sleep for a little while?

GRAN: Why do you want me to sleep if I'm going to be sleeping the eternal sleep in not too long? *(She laughs until she is overcome by coughing.)* Like Margarita. Did you hear about Margarita, Gonzalito? Did you tell him, Rita?

MAMA RITA: No, Mama.

GRAN: It must have been in the papers. Wasn't it, Gonzalito?

GONZALO: *(Abruptly stops reading)* No, it wasn't.

GRAN: *(Smiles with satisfaction)* Well, just imagine. Margarita, the cripple, remember? The one who had her head shaved. The crazy one.

GONZALO: Yeah, yeah.

GRAN:　Well, Margarita, the one from the market, the other day came to visit me and said that if I wanted, she'd do my shopping for me, buy my papaya, my fruit. You know how much fruit I eat.

MAMA RITA:　Fruit! There's no fruit!

GRAN:　So. . .

ALBERTO:　It's OK, Mama. We don't need fruit.

GRAN:　*(Pouting)*　So, since I don't have anyone to do any shopping for me. . .

MAMA RITA:　You go, Alberto.

ALBERTO:　No, Mama, not right now.

MAMA RITA:　Tell Gonzalo to loan you the car.

GONZALO:　He doesn't know how to drive.

ALBERTO:　Hey, Mr. know-it-all.

GONZALO:　Calm down, John Lennon.

MAMA RITA:　Sweetheart, loan him your car.

GRAN:　That's dangerous, Rita. He's just a boy.

MAMA RITA:　No one asked you, Mama.

ALBERTO:　I won't go.

MAMA RITA:　You're going, with or without the car.

ALBERTO:　I won't go.

GONZALO:　It's your fault. Keep on overprotecting your son like you do and you'll see.

MAMA RITA:　Come on, Albertito.

ALBERTO:　No.

MAMA RITA:　If you all want to eat everyone has to pitch in.

ALBERTO:　No one asked you to prepare a big dinner.

GRAN:　If I could walk, I'd go. That's one of the bad things about getting old.

MAMA RITA:　Mama, no one is asking you to do anything. Don't start.

GRAN:　I know, but I don't want to freeload, either. If I'm invited I want to do something. At least wash the dishes.

MAMA RITA:　Yeah, and then you'll get sick and we'll have to call the doctor and pay for the medicine.

GRAN:　Look, Rita, what I've got is never going away. *(She shows her hands to an absent audience.)* Rheumatoid arthritis is incurable.

MAMA RITA:　Don't get morbid, Mama.

GRAN: It's the truth.

GONZALO: We can have a good time without fruit, can't we?

MAMA RITA: Well, then you'll have to make do with the cake from the bakery.

GRAN: Ooh, the one I like! It's the one made with wine in it, isn't it, Gonzalito?

GONZALO: No, it's the mocha one.

GRAN: No, it's the one with wine in it.

GONZALO: Hm.

GRAN: *(She gets up with difficulty.)* I'm going to the kitchen.

MAMA RITA: Sit down, Mama, everything's all ready. I've been up since seven this morning.

GRAN: I'm going to see what else needs to be done.

ALBERTO: Leave her alone. Granny-Granma's going to look at the cake.

GRAN: *(Offended)* No, I'm not, son, something stinks in the kitchen.

GONZALO: *(Laughs)* It's the cabbage dinner.

GRAN: Don't pick on your mother, Gonzalo. *(He goes out through the door that goes to the kitchen.)*

MAMA RITA: Alberto, put on some music.

GONZALO: Shall we open the wine?

> *Alberto goes to the stereo and turns it on. We hear "Let's Stay Together," sung by Tina Turner. During this scene he will imitate a guitarist playing to the rhythm of the music. From time to time he will issue some muffled shouts and will twist around like a rock star in concert.*

GONZALO: *(Goes to the dining room and takes a bottle of white wine that is on the table.)* Where's the corkscrew?

MAMA RITA: On the table.

GONZALO: Don't we have a corkscrew?

MAMA RITA: It's on the kitchen table.

Gonzalo exits through the door which leads to the kitchen. He is muttering something.

MAMA RITA: *(Knitting mechanically. She talks distractedly to Alberto.)* What's it called?
ALBERTO: *(Absorbed by the music)* What?
MAMA RITA: The song.
ALBERTO: "Let's Stay Together."
MAMA RITA: Turn it down a little.

Gonzalo comes in through the kitchen door. He uncorks the bottle. He sneezes. He pours the wine in three glasses, which he puts on the coffee table in the living room.

GONZALO: Last week I had a chance to buy an excellent German wine.
MAMA RITA: So why didn't you buy it?

Granny-Granma enters through the kitchen door eating bits of fried pigskin and she tries to move to the rhythm of the music. She pretends she has an audience.

GRAN: Too bad I can't move anymore.
MAMA RITA: It's gonna be even harder if you keep eating the way you do, Mama.
GRAN: *(Offended)* It's just a piece of old pork rind I found rotting in a corner.
GONZALO: *(Drinks his wine down hurriedly. He pours himself more.)* I'm going to tell Jimenez to get me at least two bottles.

Alberto goes to the coffee table and picks up his glass, drinks a few swallows. Mama Rita does the same.

GRAN: *(Goes to the living room, always eating and making noises with her mouth. She sits.)* I eat any old thing, or rather, whatever is left over. You can't tell me I come over here to eat up your food. I hardly eat anything. That's why my stomach is shrinking. I've been on a diet for twenty years. You know that, Rita.

> *Knock at the door. Gonzalo goes to open it. Enter Silvia.*

MAMA RITA: That's enough, Mama.
GONZALO: *(To Silvia)* Hey there.
SILVIA: *(Moving quickly)* Hello, all. *(She goes up the stairs.)*
GRAN: She's gotta go, bad.

> *Silvia exits.*

MAMA RITA: Mama, I want you to calm down. No one is being mean to you, so don't you be mean either.
GRAN: You inherited your father's character. I'm not doing anything.
MAMA RITA: Stop interfering with other people's lives. I have enough problems without you and your silliness.
GRAN: Just because I said that Silvia had to go to the bathroom. That's not being mean. We all have our needs.
MAMA RITA: You know what I'm talking about. *(She goes to the stereo and turns it off.)* I'd like us all to be happy today.
GRAN: We old people get blamed for everything. We stink, we're in the way, we eat too much. . . I have no desire to bother anyone.
MAMA RITA: You know what I'm talking about.
GRAN: No, I don't know.
ALBERTO: *(Violently)* Stop it, you two. I hate all this negative stuff.
GRAN: Graciela's children want to send her to an old folks' home. I think that's good. Of course, after that, you die right away.
GONZALO: Hardy weeds are hard to kill.
GRAN: Who are you referring to, son? Because, with you as the doctor, they'll die after the first visit.
ALBERTO: That's the way all doctors are, Granny-Granma.

GRAN: They're the worst murderers there are.

> *Silvia comes down the stairs. She goes*
> *to the living room and sits down.*

MAMA RITA: How were your classes?

SILVIA: Fine. Did you all know that Mama Rita is interested in Psychology?

GONZALO: Your crazy ideas have rubbed off on her.

MAMA RITA: Did you bring me the book?

SILVIA: I didn't go to the library. I'll bring it to you tomorrow.

> *Alberto gets restless. He starts to hum*
> *the song "Mother" by John Lennon.*

MAMA RITA: Well, everyone's brain needs a little dusting off at some point.

GRAN: My little girl. Silvia. *(She laughs maliciously.)* No one even remembers us old people anymore, do they?

SILVIA: I said "hi," Granny-Granma.

GRAN: You look good, Silvia. Like always, I'm sick.

MAMA RITA: Well, now if only your father would get here, and Kiqui.

GONZALO: That pair! Kiqui hasn't even taken the trouble to look us up.

MAMA RITA: Gonzalo, I don't know what's gotten into you today!

ALBERTO: It's that time of the month for him.

> *Granny-Granma laughs. They all look*
> *at her disapprovingly.*

GRAN: Old people are in the way. Last night I was thinking about that. You know what, Rita? I dreamed about your father. Maybe he's calling me.

MAMA RITA: Don't start the guilt trip, Mama.

GRAN: I'm not. It's just that everything hurts me. Silvia, would you believe that even my toes are swollen? Some days, Rita, it really gets me down.

MAMA RITA: Mama, what did you expect? It's natural to have pains. You're not a spring chicken anymore.

GRAN: Well, that's what I dreamed. That your father was calling me.

Knock at the door. Alberto goes to open it.

GONZALO: You never want to take the right medicine.

GRAN: Hm.

Enter Kiqui. She hugs Alberto.

KIQUI: Little brother! Don't you look good!

ALBERTO: Hey there!

KIQUI: *(Goes to Mama Rita)* Mommy, sweet mommy, you look divine! Absolutely beautiful!

MAMA RITA: Really? How was the trip?

KIQUI: Fine. You look wonderful. How did you manage to start looking younger? You must be in love. Love rejuvenates.

MAMA RITA: *(Laughing, pleased)* I made cabbage dinner. *(They kiss each other.)*

KIQUI: Yum, delicious! Home, sweet home! *(She goes to Gonzalo.)* And how's my little grumpy brother? Handsome! *(She kisses him.)* With that mustache I feel a little incest coming on.

GONZALO: *(Putting his arm around her waist)* Same to you, Kiqui. You look beautiful!

KIQUI : *(Going toward Silvia)* And Silvia? A real professional now! *(She goes to Granny-Granma)* Granny-Granma, you look so good, so rosy-cheeked and healthy. . .

GRAN: *(Smiles, pleased)* Maybe because I'm about to die.

KIQUI: Oh, Granny! Where's Dad?

MAMA RITA: He'll be here any minute. Sit down, Kiqui. Tell us everything.

KIQUI: Everything? No, no, no. You all tell me everything.

GONZALO: *(Very gentleman-like)* A glass of wine, mademoiselle?

MAMA RITA: Yes, let's toast. Get some more glasses, Alberto.

ALBERTO: Why do I have to do everything?

MAMA RITA: Come on, don't show your colors.

GRAN: *(To Kiqui)* Honey, I can't even walk anymore.

KIQUI: Oh, no, Granny!

*Alberto puts the glasses on the coffee
table and serves the wine.*

ALBERTO: Do you want some, Granny?
GRAN: I don't drink, Albie. When I get to heaven, the Lord is going
to send me down below for being so boring. I don't drink, I
don't smoke, I don't do anything.
ALBERTO: Not even a little green stuff?
GRAN: *(Laughs)* Yeah, I do that.
MAMA RITA: Well, now, let's all say: cheers!

They all say "cheers!"

GRAN: I'll toast with milk.
ALBERTO: Why don't you just use an empty glass?
MAMA RITA: Mama, don't be silly.
GRAN: That won't do. I want milk in my glass. *(She goes to the
kitchen.)*
KIQUI: *(Raising her glass)* I propose a toast to everyone.
GONZALO: *(Doing the same)* I toast to Kiqui. I hope she finds
herself someday.
ALBERTO: Jerk.
MAMA RITA: To our all being together. To all my children.

They all applaud.

ALBERTO: How did you manage to produce Gonzalo, Mama? He
looks like a product of a rape.
GONZALO: And you were bought when the factory was going out of
business.

*Granny-Granma enters with a glass of
milk in her hand.*

MAMA RITA: All my children are precious.
SILVIA: Especially the guys.
KIQUI: *(Sarcastically)* Oh, yeah.
GRAN: *(Raising her glass)* Cheers, everyone.
KIQUI: *(Half-heartedly)* Cheers, Granny-Granma.

MAMA RITA: Is it past three already?
GONZALO: Yep.

Granny-Granma drinks her glass of milk.

ALBERTO: I hope that doesn't go to your head, Granny-Granma.
SILVIA: I think she's hungry.
GONZALO: You're going to get indigestion.
GRAN: I can't have any fun.   Old people are always sad, but when
we start to have a little fun. . .
MAMA RITA: That's enough, Mama.
GONZALO: We're expecting Dad, aren't we?
KIQUI: Yeah, what's up?
GRAN: *(Quickly)*   You remember Margarita, don't you, Kiqui?   The
crippled woman?
KIQUI: *(Disappointed)*   Sure.
GRAN: Well, the other day. . . you know how she lives in the street
and doesn't have any place to relieve herself and all that, well,
she went to take a shower at the public baths, there in the
market.   They have some showers right there in the market. . .
KIQUI: Yeah?

*The telephone rings.   Mama Rita goes
to answer it.*

GONZALO: I'm not here.
MAMA RITA: *(Into the phone)*   Well, yes, just a moment, please.
Alberto.
GONZALO: *(To Kiqui)*   Did you know that Alberto is trying to get
a girlfriend?
ALBERTO: *(Goes to telephone)*   You're crazy!

*Everyone becomes silent to listen to
Alberto.*

ALBERTO: *(Into the phone)*   Yeah, uh-huh, no, ok, bye. *(He hangs
up.)*
KIQUI: You sound like a donkey!   What a way to talk on the phone!
GONZALO: He thinks he's being cool.
ALBERTO: Shut up, asshole!
MAMA RITA: *(Conciliatory)*   That's enough, children.

GRAN: Ah, in my times. We knew what courtship was. Your grandfather sent me letters. Of course, I think he copied them all from different poets, but. . .

MAMA RITA: *(Sarcastic)*   That's why you had such a good marriage.

GRAN: You may not think so. But it was better the old way. Not like now, when you get married, unmarried. . .

GONZALO: It's better now.

KIQUI: Gonzalo should know.

GONZALO: You're not far behind. Am I wrong? What does the psychologist of the family think?

SILVIA: You can't really say that the way things are done now is. . . well, before, there was a different idea about "fidelity."

GRAN: At least your grandfather put a lot of effort into it. He used to send me letters.

MAMA RITA: You were crazy about him. He was your Clark Gable. How disgusting.

GRAN: There are worse things.

GONZALO: Like when Kiqui ran away with the bald guy.

MAMA RITA: That's enough, Gonzalo.

KIQUI: It's OK, Mama. If everybody hadn't been so straight-laced and up-tight it wouldn't have even been a problem. . . well, it would have been worse if I'd married him.

GONZALO: There are no morals anymore.

KIQUI: Hey, Gonzalito! No one criticized you about Maria Elena. And you're supposed to be the man of the family.

GONZALO: I got married.

GRAN: That's right. He did. He got married.

KIQUI: You got married. You got unmarried. You got married again. And now you're separated. That's bad.   Especially if it's with the same person.

ALBERTO: It's because he's monogamous.

GONZALO: Go jerk off!

MAMA RITA: Gonzalo, what bad taste!

ALBERTO: All proctologists have bad taste.

SILVIA: It goes with the profession.

KIQUI: You mean he's projecting?

SILVIA: No worse than the rest of you.

KIQUI: I don't understand how you can say you're a psychologist. I really can't understand it. Don't you know there is such a thing as sexual preference?

SILVIA: I studied that in my first year.

KIQUI: OK, then, you draw the conclusions.

GONZALO: *(Sneezes)* That's right, draw the conclusions. The girl runs away from home. She leaves with her lover, the bald man.

ALBERTO: *(Humming)* "She is leaving home, bye, bye. . ."

GONZALO: She decides to go off to Venezuela to be an actress. And now she lives with some little second-rate director. And that makes her real liberal.

KIQUI: It's not that I'm not liberal. I'm consistent.

GONZALO: Consistent?

MAMA RITA: Shut up, all of you! None of you knows anything about anything. *(She looks at her watch.)* Your father shouldn't be much longer. *(She gets up and goes through the door leading to the kitchen.)*

KIQUI: Say what you will, I'm consistent with myself.

GONZALO: You're starting to look sort of scared.

ALBERTO: Kiqui acts like somebody really straight.

KIQUI: Scared? Please! Let me tell you something. . . *(She looks at Granny-Granma.)* If Granny-Granma weren't here. . .

GRAN: *(Proudly)* There's nothing I haven't already heard. Go ahead. You can talk in front of me.

KIQUI: Do you think I'm afraid of other kinds of experiences?

ALBERTO: Cover your ears, Gran.

GRAN: You see everything in the movies, now, son. The other day, that morbid Azucena Franco, my neighbor, went to see a movie called something like "one on top of the other."

GONZALO: They also show sex with animals.

KIQUI: Or totally censored movies. Repressed.

SILVIA: Yeah, where the man and woman give each other one kiss at the end of the movie and they don't even feel anything. That's frigidity.

GRAN: I never had that. But I think I told you how your grandfather was impotent on our honeymoon. And my horrible mother-in-law wanted me to go visit one of the peasants. A big black man, if you'd only seen him. . .

KIQUI: You would have had more fun.

SILVIA: In psychology that's called. . .

KIQUI: You talk pure theory, Silvia.

GRAN: Get yourself a boyfriend, Silvia.

GONZALO: Stop criticizing.

SILVIA: That'll never happen. I'm not going to have a boyfriend.

KIQUI: See a psychologist.

GONZALO: Look who's talking.

KIQUI: I don't believe in that stuff. There are no explanations for the way things are. I don't have to see a psychoanalyst in order to do what I want.

SILVIA: A psychologist isn't the same as a psychoanalyst.

KIQUI: It's the same thing.

GONZALO: Don't be retarded.

GRAN: It's the same thing.

ALBERTO: The other day I heard Gonzalo talking to Maria Elena. *(She imitates Gonzalo:)* Look here, sweetie. I'm your little caboose. Let's see if a doctor can fix your springs and in the meantime maybe my spirits will be a little higher more frequently.

> *Gonzalo gets up and throws himself at Alberto. He takes him by the shoulders and pushes him. Alberto falls wildly onto Granny-Granma.*

KIQUI: Stop clowning around!

GRAN: Go play outside! *(She is overcome by a coughing fit.)*

SILVIA: Did they hurt you, Gran?

GRAN: *(Exaggerating her cough)* No, no, dear. It's just that my lungs aren't any good anymore.

> *Alberto and Gonzalo separate. Later, Alberto looks for another confrontation with Gonzalo, but Gonzalo avoids it.*

ALBERTO: Let's see who's stronger.

GONZALO: Calm down. Calm down.

> *The telephone rings. Silvia goes to
> answer it.*

SILVIA: *(Into the telephone)* Hello. Hello. *(The caller hangs up.)*
No one answers.

GRAN: *(Tries to get up, with difficulty)* They still act like kids.
They should be more considerate. . . *(She goes toward the
kitchen, exits.)*

GONZALO: *(To Alberto)* You want me to beat you up?

ALBERTO: Shut up, Dumbo!

KIQUI: *(Amused)* You almost killed Granny-Granma.

> *They all laugh.*

SILVIA: You squashed her and stepped on her.

> *Granny-Granma enters from the
> kitchen. She moves quietly toward the
> living room.*

ALBERTO: Gonzalo pushed me.

GRAN: I knew it! Rita's in a bad mood. *(She goes toward the
kitchen again. She is muttering something.)*

ALBERTO: You guys love to exaggerate. *(He climbs the stairs and
exits.)*

> *Gonzalo starts reading the paper
> again. The phone rings. Silvia goes to
> answer it.*

SILVIA: *(Into the phone)* Hello, hello. *(She hangs up.)* They're not
hanging up.

MAMA RITA'S VOICE: *(From the kitchen)* Kiqui! Kiqui!

> *Kiqui gets up lazily and goes to the
> kitchen. She exits.*

SILVIA: They're not hanging up.

GONZALO: What?

SILVIA: Somebody calls and stays on the line, but they won't answer.

GONZALO: If they call again, I'll answer.

SILVIA: I doubt it's for you.

> *The telephone rings again. Silvia and Gonzalo look at each other. He goes to answer it.*

GONZALO: *(Into the phone)* Hello, hello? *(He hangs up.)* Somebody's playing around.

SILVIA: Children love to play telephone. That's because they love to imitate their parents. *(She gets up and goes to the bookcase. She caresses the spines of the books.)*

> *Gonzalo goes to the bar and takes out some bottles of imported liquor.*

SILVIA: This *Don Quijote* book is really old.

> *Kiqui comes in from the kitchen, carrying a pitcher of lemonade. She puts it on the table.*

KIQUI: Mama's in a great mood. *(She goes back into the kitchen.)*

GONZALO: Spanish brandy or cognac. Which do you prefer?

SILVIA: Those belong to Dad!

> *Granny-Granma enters from the kitchen, carrying with her a basket of bread. She places it on the table.*

GRAN: What a snit your mother's in! She can't even stand herself!

GONZALO: Don't be a terrorist, Granny-Granma.

> *Kiqui and Mama Rita enter from the kitchen. Kiqui is carrying a soup tureen, which she places on the table.*

MAMA RITA: Come to the table, Mama.

20

Granny-Granma sits down at the table.

MAMA RITA: The soup is hot. Albertito! Albertito! Come on down and eat.

ALBERTO'S VOICE: I'm in the bathroom!

GONZALO: *(Sarcastically)* I told you so. What all does he do in the bathroom? He stays in there forever. *(He goes to sit at the table.)*

MAMA RITA: Let's have a little peace while we eat. There's no reason for you to be fighting like this.

GONZALO: Shouldn't we wait for Dad?

KIQUI: It's really late. I'm hungry. I say we start. The soup smells delicious. *(She begins to serve the bowls of soup. Mama Rita and Silvia also sit down at the table. They begin to eat.)*

GRAN: Just a little for me.

MAMA RITA: You all better eat up, enjoy it now, because I'm on the point of declaring myself on strike. I'm sick of cooking.

GONZALO: You've been saying that for as long as I've known you.

MAMA RITA: But this time I mean it. Alberto!

A little later Alberto appears. He comes down the stairs. The phone rings. Alberto answers it.

ALBERTO: *(Into the phone)* Hello, hello. *(He hangs up.)* What's the hurry? *(He goes to the table and sits down.)*

GONZALO: Your eyes got all red while you were in the bathroom.

KIQUI: The soup's getting cold, Alberto. Serve yourself. You're not expecting me to wait on you, are you?

Alberto serves himself some soup.

SILVIA: Pass the bread, Gonzalo.

GRAN: Well I told you all about Margarita, didn't I? The poor thing used to take her bath in the baths at the market and one day, they say she took a long time, it was Wednesday of last week. Well, in those baths they just give them ten minutes to get in there and out again and they say she had been in there more than a half hour. . .

MAMA RITA: And what are your plans, Kiqui?

KIQUI: I just signed a contract for a movie of Mario Argudin's, a man I met down there. He's pretty well-known. I'm going to play the part of a Mexican woman. They pay well.

ALBERTO: The soup is salty.

MAMA RITA: Tough!

SILVIA: I'd say it needs more salt.

MAMA RITA: Gonzalito's going to Japan. To take a course, right, son?

GONZALO: Yeah.

KIQUI: Oh.

SILVIA: *(To Alberto)* Pass the salt.

Alberto hands her the salt shaker.

GRAN: Silvia says she doesn't ever want a boyfriend.

KIQUI: The movie's not bad. I'm sort of a flaky girl who falls in love with a drug trafficker and they end up killing me.

ALBERTO: After ten minutes?

KIQUI: The drug trafficker has another woman, but he's really in love with me. Of course, I'm sort of like his lover. We've already shot the first scene. I'm walking down the main street in Caracas, and a guy is following me. I realize it and I run away.

GONZALO: I wouldn't pay money to see you run away.

KIQUI: There are lots of scenes. But all of the others are shot inside.

GONZALO: On the bed, at the beach, in the bathroom.

GRAN: Not at the beach. She said inside. Although they could take sand into the studio and let them roll around on it there.

MAMA RITA: Mama, I told you that if you want to eat with us you'll have to keep your mouth shut!

GRAN: I know, I know. You act like I'm your enemy.

MAMA RITA: You are.

KIQUI: I can't believe you are all so ignorant.

SILVIA: Don't pay any attention to them. They don't know that some nude scenes are very artistic.

Gonzalo laughs sarcastically.

KIQUI: *(To Silvia)* Shut up, you old nun.

> *The telephone rings.   Granny-Granma*
> *goes to answer it.*

MAMA RITA: I don't know why you talk to each other like this. You're not children anymore.

SILVIA: Somebody gave me a little spoon.

GRAN: *(Into the phone)* Hello? I can't hear anything. Answer me! You dirty dogs! *(She hangs up.)* They don't want to answer me, Rita. *(She goes to the table and sits down.)*

KIQUI:*(To Gonzalo)* I'll have some salad.

GONZALO: All I see is avocado.

MAMA RITA: Pass her the avocado.

> *Gonzalo passes her the avocado.*

KIQUI: *(To Gonzalo)* You act like a little child. It's time you let go of mother's apron strings.

MAMA RITA: Leave me out of this.

> *The telephone rings.*

MAMA RITA: I'll get it. *(She goes to answer.)*

SILVIA: Did she cook up any beans?

GRAN: No, dear, your mother doesn't like to cook anymore. *(She makes a face as if the soup were terrible.)*

MAMA RITA: *(Into the phone)* Hello, yes, that's right. Now look. *(Pause.)* No. Yes, but. . . Fine! Good-bye! *(She hangs up violently. She exits toward the kitchen.)*

> *A long silence.*

GRAN: *(Entering into complicity with the others)* I told you so.

KIQUI: Eat your soup, Gran.

GRAN: Your belly shrinks if you don't eat. Imagine what mine must be like. Besides, you young people can eat all kinds of garbage and it doesn't affect you. *(Smiling toward an absent audience.)*

> *The telephone rings, Mama Rita hurries to enter from the kitchen. She answers it.*

MAMA RITA: *(Her voice lowered)* Yes, yes, we've met. Yes, I know. They're all crazy. I told you that this morning. No. He'll be here later. Do whatever you want to do! *(Hangs up. She sits back down at the table.)* That was your father. He's not coming to dinner.

> *There is an uncomfortable silence.*

GONZALO: Did something happen?
MAMA RITA: Just that your father's not coming to dinner. He has a meeting.

> *Silence. Gonzalo sneezes.*

KIQUI: Tomorrow before I leave for the airport I'll call him or come over.
GONZALO: *(To Mama Rita)* Aren't you going to eat?
GRAN: Your soup came out good. *(She tries to get by.)* I'll get the cabbage dinner.
MAMA RITA: Everybody sit down! I'll serve the cabbage.

> *Granny-Granma sits down again quickly, but she loses her balance and half falls out of her chair. She remains with her head down around her feet, trying to straighten up, for a good while. No one helps her. The telephone rings. They all look at each other.*

MAMA RITA: Don't answer!

> *Mama Rita continues to eat. The telephone keeps ringing insistently.*

KIQUI: Mm, my mouth is watering.

MAMA RITA: I'm coming. I don't have any servants, you know.

GRAN: *(From her fallen position)* It was your favorite meal when
      you were little, Kiqui.

MAMA RITA: Stop clowning around! Get up!

GRAN: I can't Rita.

> *Alberto brusquely helps Granny-*
> *Granma get up.*

GRAN: Did you hear my back crack? *(No one looks at her. She
smiles toward an absent audience.)*

> *The telephone stops ringing.   There is*
> *an uncomfortable silence.*

MAMA RITA: I'll get the dinner. *(She exits through the kitchen
      door.)*

KIQUI: Don't get Mama Rita mad, now.

ALBERTO: You started it.

KIQUI: Me?

GONZALO: That's right. Stop talking about your stupid cabbage
      dinner.

KIQUI: You're an ass.

SILVIA: We should talk about something pleasant. Something that
      would relieve our tensions.

GRAN: If you want anything, you have to serve yourselves.

SILVIA: Stop trying to attract attention, Granny.

> *Mama Rita comes in with a platter of*
> *cabbage. She begins to dish it into the*
> *plates.*

MAMA RITA: Eat every bite of it, all of you. You, too, Gonzalo.

> *Gonzalo sneezes.*

MAMA RITA: Take the dirty plates to the kitchen, Alberto.

ALBERTO: *(With quick, agile movements he gathers the dirty plates and says sarcastically)* Sure, sure. Here we all help out. There aren't any servants. *(He exits through the kitchen door.)*

> *Mama Rita follows Alberto. She exits.*

SILVIA: Let's talk about pleasant things.
GRAN: Pass me a tortilla, Gonzalito.

> *Gonzalo hands her the tortillas. He sneezes. Alberto enters through the kitchen door. He sits down. Mama Rita immediately appears with a napkin holder.*

MAMA RITA: What are you using to wipe your mouths? Nobody even missed the napkins. The tablecloth is brand new. Did everybody hear me?
> *There is an uncomfortable silence.*

GRAN: OK, start talking. . .
ALBERTO: The Jeans have a new record out.
SILVIA: I don't understand anything about rock.
ALBERTO: You have to follow its evolution since Elvis.
KIQUI: Since before that.
ALBERTO: OK, since Otis.
KIQUI: Don't you like Lou?
ALBERTO: Sure, I like Lou.
GONZALO: And B.B.
KIQUI: B.B. is blues.
GONZALO: Naturally.
KIQUI: OK, first Billie, Lightning, B.B., Dypree and Otis. Then, Elvis, Lou, Janis. . .

> *Mama Rita gets up suddenly and goes to the kitchen.*

SILVIA: She's suffering from tension that is generated by. . .
KIQUI: Shut up, Silvia!

SILVIA: See? Hypersensitivity.

KIQUI: So did something happen?

GRAN: Who knows? Your chatter made her nervous. All that B.B., Bobby--that's not very pleasant.

GONZALO: They had a fight.

ALBERTO: Of course they had a fight. They fight all the time. I should know--I live here.

GRAN: *(Trying to stand up)* I'll go see your mother.

GONZALO: Sit down.

KIQUI: Yeah, Gran. Stop being a pest.

GRAN: Hmm, this always happens. Your grandfather was the same way. He was always standing me up. Of course, after a while it didn't bother me. As if love were forever anyway. I don't know why Rita gets upset.

ALBERTO: *(Pouring himself more lemonade)*   You're you and mom's who she is.

SILVIA: Granny-Granma is just giving her opinion. She's trying to lower the anxiety level around here.

> *From the kitchen the noise of a plate breaking is heard. There is a silence.*

GRAN: That's why I wanted to go into the kitchen. I knew it. Rita's like that. She's not a good cook. But what do you expect, I kept her out of the kitchen when she was a girl so she wouldn't have to start suffering so young.

KIQUI: That first call wasn't from Dad.

GONZALO: Apparently not.

SILVIA: Stop interpreting.

KIQUI: Silvia, you're such a jerk.

> *Mama Rita enters, bringing with her a tray with a teapot and cups.*

GRAN: *(Clearing her throat)* I was telling you all that Margarita ended up flat out in the market bathrooms. Naked and wet.

MAMA RITA: I'm going to serve everyone their coffee *now*. I don't want to be getting up and down.

GRAN: Good. I'd like a little coffee now. I like to drink it while I eat. Albertito, pour me a cup. I can't. *(She shows her hands.)* I don't have any strength in them. Look what the arthritis has done.

> *Alberto pours a cup of coffee for Granny-Granma.*

GONZALO: *(To Alberto)* I'd like some lemonade.

> *Alberto begrudgingly pours him a glass.*

MAMA RITA: *(Breathing deeply)* I broke one of the good plates.

GONZALO: *(Trying to please)* Well, it just so happens I was planning on buying you another set. The wife of one of my doctor friends sells some beautiful sets. Japanese.

GRAN: Ugh! Those don't last anytime at all.

KIQUI: In Venezuela they make beautiful ceramic dishes.

SILVIA: Better than the ones from Cuernavaca?

GONZALO: We should take Kiqui to Cuernavaca.

KIQUI: I'd love that! But I can't. Day after tomorrow I have to film another scene. I only came back to Mexico because Mario, my director, told me it was good for my character. He said: "Go so you can be flooded by experiences."

> *The telephone rings twice. Everyone tenses up. They look at each other, cough, Gonzalo sneezes. Mama Rita gets up and goes into the kitchen.*

GONZALO: We've either got to answer the phone or disconnect it.

SILVIA: Or turn in down.

KIQUI: *(To Gonzalo)* Ask Mama Rita what's bothering her.

GONZALO: You ask her.

GRAN: It has to do with her marriage.

GONZALO: The other day when I came to eat I thought she seemed a little strange, too.

KIQUI: You come to eat a lot?

ALBERTO: He's got "Mom-itis." Ever since Maria Elena broke up with him, he's been doing a real about-face. And Mama likes it.

> *Gonzalo gets up from his chair and goes to Alberto. He takes him by the shoulders and lifts him to his feet. They start kicking each other. They do all of this without making any noise.*

KIQUI: You stooges!
GRAN: Keep your fighting quiet. Don't let Rita hear.
ALBERTO: You fight like an old lady.
GONZALO: I'm trying to teach you how.

> *Gonzalo hits him in the testicles. Alberto doubles over and whines. Kiqui gets up and tries to help Alberto. They hear noises in the kitchen. Gonzalo, Alberto and Kiqui go to their places and sit down. Alberto continues to whine. Mama Rita enters. She sits down.*

GRAN: *(To Silvia)* Your grandfather was something else.
ALBERTO: *(To Kiqui)* Pass me a napkin.
KIQUI: They're right next to you.

> *Alberto blows his nose on the napkin.*

MAMA RITA: *(To Alberto)* What's the matter with you?
GRAN: *(Angry)* Gonzalo hit him.

> *The phone rings. Mama Rita gets up from the table and goes into the kitchen.*
>
> Alberto gets up and goes to Gonzalo's place. He grabs Gonzalo by the hair and pulls as

> hard as he can. Then he escapes from
> Gonzalo and sits down at his place.

ALBERTO: You son of a . . !

GRAN: Rita's very nervous. Why don't you disconnect the phone?

KIQUI: I'll disconnect it! I've had enough! *(She goes toward the phone with determination.)* Hello! Hello! What? You've got the wrong number. Dumb broad! *(She hangs up.)* They were trying to call the "cleaning clinic." *(She goes and sits down at the table.)*

GRAN: That's why I wanted to stay home. I get so nervous these days.

> *There is a knock at the door. Gonzalo rushes to open it.*

SILVIA: Maybe it's Dad.

GRAN: At my age everything affects me, Silvia. Every day I take a pill for my heart. For the last six years.

> *Gonzalo, at the door, accepts a package. He signs a receipt and gives the messenger a tip. In the dining room everyone is waiting curiously. While this is happening, Granny-Granma continues to speak.*

GRAN: Six years taking a little pill every day. It's white, little bitty, sort of insignificant. But it's like gasoline for my heart. They say the price of gas goes up every day. Just imagine, Silvia, what I've spent on little pills. A fortune! Because I also have to buy some for my arthritis and my ulcer.

> *Gonzalo puts the package on the coffee table.*

GONZALO: *(Confidentially)* A little gift.

ALBERTO: See who it's for.

GONZALO: *(Examining the envelope)* It doesn't say. The envelope is sealed.

ALBERTO: Open it.
KIQUI: Open it.

> *Mama Rita enters through the kitchen door.*

GONZALO: A package just came.
MAMA RITA: *(She goes to the coffee table and opens the package with a child-like excitement.)* I wonder what it could be. I'll bet it's something totally useless. *(Takes the envelope attached to the package and hides it in the pocket of her dress. She finishes unpacking and finds a prehispanic clay idol.)* It's for decoration.
KIQUI: Do you think it's authentic?
GONZALO: If it's authentic it must have cost a fortune.
MAMA RITA: *(Takes it into her arms like a mother holds a baby and lulls him to sleep.)* It's just a decoration.
KIQUI: Who sent it?
MAMA RITA: Hmm? Oh, it must be from one of your father's clients. They always send useless things.
KIQUI: Open the envelope.
MAMA RITA: Your father might get angry.
KIQUI: Big deal, open it.
MAMA RITA: *(Opens the envelope and reads it to herself.)* It's from someone named J.F.
KIQUI: But what does it say?
MAMA RITA: It says: greetings, J.F.
KIQUI: What a mysterious guy!
MAMA RITA: Let's finish eating. *(She leaves the idol on the coffee table. She sits down at the table.)*
SILVIA: It looks Olmecan.
GONZALO: No, it's Mayan.
KIQUI: I think it's a beautiful gift.
MAMA RITA: *(Discouraged)* It's just for decoration.

> *A knock at the door. Mama Rita gets up to answer. When she opens the door, she goes out abruptly, closing the door behind her.*

KIQUI: Now what?
SILVIA: I'll bet it's Dad.
GRAN: It makes me nervous.
SILVIA: They must be fighting outside.
ALBERTO: You're wrong. They always fight in front of everybody.
GRAN: That's true. Last month when I was here they even involved
　　me in their quarrel.

> *Gonzalo gets up and goes to the window
> which overlooks the street. Kiqui
> follows him. They look through the
> window.*

GONZALO: I think that car belongs to Gonzalez Marquez.
KIQUI: The lawyer?
GRAN: I'm too old for these things.
KIQUI: He just got out of the car.
GRAN: Who?
GONZALO: I think it's. . . yeah, it's Gonzalez Marquez.
ALBERTO: Some car he drives, huh?

> *There is a knock at the door. Gonzalo
> opens it. Mama Rita enters and goes
> toward the table. Kiqui and Gonzalo
> follow her.*

KIQUI: Who was it?
MAMA RITA: Gonzalez Marquez.
GONZALO: Why didn't he come in?
MAMA RITA: He was in a hurry.
KIQUI: Mama Rita, tell us what happened.
MAMA RITA: Well. . . we wanted to sell the properties in
　　Cuernavaca.
GONZALO: You mean our inheritance? I was going to build on one
　　of them.
MAMA RITA: *(Evasive)* The truth is, your father and I are getting a
　　divorce. Are you happy now? Somebody gather up the dirty
　　dishes.

Silence.

KIQUI: What else?

MAMA RITA: We raised you all, we gave you good educations, you can't complain.

KIQUI: What else?

MAMA RITA: That's it.

KIQUI: What else?

GRAN: *(To Silvia)* Sweetheart, in that bread basket there's a piece of sweetbread. *(Pause)* I like to dunk it in my coffee. *(She smiles toward an absent audience.)*

> *Silvia doesn't hear her. She passes her the sugar bowl.*

GRAN: *(Takes the sugar bowl and continues to stare)*   Thanks, sweetheart.

MAMA RITA: That's all.

KIQUI: Why?

GONZALO: What are the reasons?

GRAN: All married people have their reasons.

KIQUI: Who was the first phone call from?

MAMA RITA: Is this an interrogation?

KIQUI: Who called?

MAMA RITA: A girl friend.

KIQUI: Whose girl friend?

> *Mama Rita gets up and takes some dirty plates from the table. She carries them to the kitchen. She exits.*

GRAN: Nora, my friend from the neighborhood, she just got divorced too. But her husband was a good-for-nothing womanizer. You don't know how my friend Nora suffered.

> *Mama Rita enters from the kitchen. She sits down at the table.*

GONZALO: Well, have you got a lawyer?

MAMA RITA: It's by mutual consent.
GONZALO: And all the possessions?
MAMA RITA: Divided by mutual consent.
GONZALO: But you have a lawyer.
MAMA RITA: Gonzalez Marquez.
KIQUI: He's not good for you. He's more a friend of Dad's than
    yours.
MAMA RITA: It's all right.
GONZALO: Why hadn't you told us anything?
MAMA RITA: We wanted to be really sure first.
GONZALO: And the land in Acapulco?
MAMA RITA: Everything will be for you all.
KIQUI: And you're getting a divorce just because.
MAMA RITA: We don't get along.
GONZALO: That's no reason.
ALBERTO: Look who's talking. You with your two divorces.
GRAN: The same thing happened with your grandfather. Right, Rita?
    But back then women were stupid.
MAMA RITA: Don't compare me to you, Ma.
GONZALO: Who called you a little while ago?
MAMA RITA: Why do you want to know?
GRAN: Stop being so mysterious.
KIQUI: It's obvious.
MAMA RITA: Obvious?
GONZALO: Yes, Mom.
SILVIA: Yes, Mom.
ALBERTO: Yeah, Mom.
GRAN: That's right, Rita.

Long silence.

MAMA RITA: Have some coffee. . . *(She pours the coffee.)*
KIQUI: *(Cautiously)* A woman. . .
MAMA RITA: A woman.
GONZALO: What's her name?
GRAN: Her name starts with J.F.!
MAMA RITA: Mother, who's side are you on?
ALBERTO: I'll bet it was Magali.
KIQUI: Who's Magali?

SILVIA: Dad's secretary.

MAMA RITA: Just a woman. I don't know her name.

GRAN: Of course it was a woman. Well, you never know anymore, which kind with which kind. You see everything. . . *(She slurps her coffee noisily.)*

MAMA RITA: Stop slurping!

GONZALO: *(With an authoritarian tone)* Naturally you're keeping the house, right? And I don't know about Gonzalez Marquez being your lawyer. Anyway, I think we should contest this.

KIQUI: Not a bad idea. It's not fair that after all these years he runs away with another woman.

MAMA RITA: I don't want you all to get involved.

KIQUI: Mom, what's the matter with you? Where's your pride?

SILVIA: You're going through a stage in which your narcissistic side is very hurt.

ALBERTO: Dad's being a real prick.

SILVIA: He's probably suffering, too. But from guilt.

ALBERTO: *(To Silvia)* That stinking traitor secretary.

GONZALO: I'm not gonna take this. He'll have to deal with me. *(He sneezes.)*

MAMA RITA: Stay out of it. We needed the fruit, didn't we?

GONZALO: Why didn't he show up to eat?

KIQUI: It's been a year since he's seen me.

MAMA RITA: He had a meeting.

KIQUI: That's a child's justification.

SILVIA: Maybe it's true.

MAMA RITA: Why do you always defend your father?

ALBERTO: 'Cause she's a nun.

GONZALO: He thinks this is gonna be easy. Over my dead body.

GRAN: When your grandfather used to abuse me, Rita couldn't defend me. Too bad I didn't have a male child. It makes a difference.

SILVIA: In every couple there's always a submissive partner and a. . .

ALBERTO: The coffee's weak.

KIQUI: You'll have to lose some weight and fix yourself up.

GONZALO: You could come to Japan with me.

KIQUI: Or come to Venezuela to visit me. I'm sure Mario would pay for it.

GONZALO: Uh-uh. That's what I'm here for. You'll have plenty of money.

ALBERTO: We'll go to the club a lot, Mom.

GONZALO: All you have to do is get organized Mom.

ALBERTO: Yeah, like Gonzalito--you get divorced and you go to your mother's house for dinner every night.

GRAN: Oh, no, I don't cook anymore, kids.

SILVIA: You could start therapy to work through the separation. I know some very qualified people.

KIQUI: Don't start with your whack-o ideas, Silvia.

GRAN: I never left your grandfather. Not that I didn't want to. These days it's better if a woman stays put. I never taught Rita anything about housekeeping.

MAMA RITA: Shut up, Ma!

Silence.

GONZALO: How long have you been like this?

MAMA RITA: A few months.

GONZALO: Months!

ALBERTO: What a bastard!

MAMA RITA: *(Goes toward the living room and sits down)* Let's move over here. *(Takes her knitting and starts to knit.)*

> They all get up except Granny-Granma, who remains seated, eating. Silvia goes to the bookcase and takes books down and puts them back. She opens them, looks at them, reads a few lines and closes them again. Gonzalo sits down and tries to put the newspaper in order. Kiqui sits down next to Mama Rita and starts to put on her make-up. Alberto sits on the arm of the chair. All of this happens while Mama Rita is talking:

MAMA RITA: Let's go over this slowly. *(Silence)* You have nothing to worry about. Your father is not a child and neither am I. Besides, for the love of God, nowadays everybody gets divorced. You all get to organize your lives and nobody

interferes. You're all grown up. You know what you're doing.
I don't want you to give me any problems about this.
Everything can be worked out by talking about it. Sooner or
later it was bound to happen. Divorce is a pretty common
topic these days.

GONZALO: But he's got the advantage over you.

SILVIA: What Mom said is very reasonable.

KIQUI: If you don't have anything interesting to say, keep your trap
shut.

SILVIA: And *you're* a mental case.

GONZALO: Dad's got no shame.

KIQUI: He's a very closed man.

ALBERTO: A hypocrite.

SILVIA: He's not a bad man. He just doesn't know how to
communicate.

KIQUI: What did he do when I went to Venezuela with Ricardo?

SILVIA: When you went whoring?

GONZALO: At least you could have married him.

KIQUI: He kicked me out of the house. He never even tried to think
of my problems.

GONZALO: He's a cheapskate.

ALBERTO: After ten at night he won't let us turn anything on--not
the TV, not the record player, not even the lights.

GONZALO: Do you know how much it cost me to finish my degree?

ALBERTO: He wants me to go to work. He doesn't want me to
study music. He doesn't want me to buy any clothes. He's
against everything.

SILVIA: That's not the problem.

KIQUI: I think you're the problem. You're a case, Silvia. When has
Dad ever given me any money? And I'm a woman.

GRAN: *(From the table)* He probably spends it all on that slut.

KIQUI: I'll never forgive him. You never know when he loves you
and when he doesn't.

ALBERTO: He never does.

GRAN: He's a very educated man. You can't deny that.

KIQUI: I don't ever remember him giving me a kiss when I was a
little girl. He never went to school to pick me up.

ALBERTO: All he ever does is yell at me.

KIQUI: He never went to any of the school events.

GONZALO: He wants everybody to be just like him.

KIQUI: You do OK. Since you're a proctologist, you're the smart one of the family.

GRAN: Some smart one! He can't even write me a prescription!

GONZALO: That's not true, Granny-Granma. You're the one who won't let me write you a prescription.

GRAN: What for? You always say there's nothing wrong with me. Even though I've got pains everywhere. Anyway, the last pills you gave me made me break out in red spots. I looked like a jelly roll.

KIQUI: He wants all of us to have respectable professions. He's so ignorant. Doesn't he realize that acting is a profession?

SILVIA: What's important is the amount of affection you get when you're a child.

ALBERTO: That's stupid. What's important is if you're understood. Dad is totally ignorant about music. He thinks rock and roll is only for drug addicts.

GRAN: That's what they say on TV.

KIQUI: He's a dictator.

SILVIA: You're exaggerating.

KIQUI: The poor man is kicking up his heels one last time. I'll bet he's making a fool of himself.

ALBERTO: That's right. He thinks he's so young. He wears sport coats that make him look like a clown.

GRAN: Old people, to the funny farm! *(She laughs maliciously.)*

MAMA RITA: Mother, stop eating! You're going to get indigestion.

GRAN: *(Still eating)* I'm not eating, Rita.

KIQUI: He's a poor soul.

ALBERTO: A corrupt pig.

MAMA RITA: Don't talk about your father like that.

KIQUI: Unfortunately, we didn't choose him.

MAMA RITA: Why do you all blame us for everything?

GONZALO: We don't, Mama Rita. The truth is that the one who's been supportive of us is you. We owe you everything.

KIQUI: Anyway, you shouldn't make excuses for him.

SILVIA: There's no need for her to speak against him, either.

GRAN: Rita had lots of boyfriends. *(Pause)* Do you remember that boy who brought you a serenade? That was the one I wanted for you. He was so outgoing. I like music, but, too late now, you got married.

KIQUI: Women today aren't like before. You can remake your life.

SILVIA: That's true. You have to relearn.

GONZALO: Don't worry about money. We're here for you.

KIQUI: What's important is that you feel young. Of course, if you help yourself, all the better. First, a little plastic surgery. . .

GRAN: In my day they didn't do that face lifting stuff. You see that now, though, on TV.

ALBERTO: Complete plastic surgery.

GONZALO: These days there's no danger involved.

KIQUI: A new hair cut, a new color.

ALBERTO: Stylish clothes.

SILVIA: Today's fashions look good on anyone. That's a very interesting psychological phenomenon.

ALBERTO: You're going to be stunning.

KIQUI: Yeah, Mom. We don't want to see any crying or staying home or anything like that.

SILVIA: That would be bad. Your period of mourning should be handled. . .

GRAN: Oh, when your grandfather died I was in mourning for five years!

KIQUI: Life goes on.

GRAN: Nothing lasts forever.

MAMA RITA: Are you finished? I don't agree with what you're saying about your father.

KIQUI: Mama Rita, don't you have any pride?

ALBERTO: That's the height of submission.

MAMA RITA: I think. . .

GRAN: That's what happened to Mariangeles. Her husband slept with everybody including the maids. Poor Mariangeles, such a lost soul.

MAMA RITA: I can't stand this! I'm being attacked right in my own house!

GRAN: *(Gets up, offended)* Look, Rita, if you didn't want to invite me, why did you? I know I'm in the way. *(She starts to whimper.)* But I'll leave right now.

MAMA RITA: Nobody's asking you to leave.

GRAN: You're throwing me out. I heard it with my own ears. Old people aren't deaf or stupid.

ALBERTO: Then stop acting like you are, Gran.

GRAN: *(To Gonzalo)* Take me home, Gonzalito. If I could walk I'd go all the way home on foot.

GONZALO: Calm down, Gran. It's OK.

GRAN: You take me, Albertito.

GONZALO: Mom, you don't realize what Dad's done to all of us. Look at Kiqui. The poor thing has become totally common. All because he didn't understand her.

SILVIA: She's afraid of success.

GONZALO: She goes from man to man.

SILVIA: She's looking for an improved father image.

KIQUI: Lay off me, will you?

GONZALO: It's true.

GRAN: You take me, Silvia. Just straight home.

KIQUI: You're more screwed up than I am.

GONZALO: And look at Alberto. Completely disoriented. He doesn't want to study, he spends all his time on pot, listening to rock.

GRAN: Let's go, Alberto.

SILVIA: He's lacking in affection.

KIQUI: And what about poor Silvia? She doesn't even have the guts to live.

GONZALO: Lonely as a dog.

SILVIA: Not as lonely as you.

KIQUI: She must have some sort of sexual trauma. And where would it come from? From her image of her father.

GRAN: Silvia, are you going to take me?

SILVIA: Sit down and stop bothering us, Granny-Granma.

MAMA RITA: Be still, Ma.

GRAN: I've been thrown out of better places. And I'm not just saying that. But I'm going home. I can never say a thing, because Rita doesn't like anything I say. It's not fair. I gave my life for her. If you raise crows they'll poke your eyes out.

ALBERTO: Gonzalo's a mess, too.

KIQUI: Absolutely. No doubt about it.

GONZALO: I'm the only responsible one in the bunch. All the weight of the family is on me.

SILVIA: Don't exaggerate.

KIQUI: Poor Gonzalo. He can't seem to find a stable relationship either.

SILVIA: He's somewhat effeminate.

GONZALO: It's all Dad's fault.

GRAN: Well, I'll just go upstairs and get my things.

> *Granny-Granma goes to the stairs. She climbs each stair slowly. When she gets halfway up she stops, agitated. She rests on the handrail.*

KIQUI: We don't want you to feel bad about all that, Mom, but it's the truth. We all agree. You need to make your life over.

GONZALO: None of us like to hear the truth.

KIQUI: Mommy, we owe everything to you. Who always did the cooking?

GONZALO: Who helped us with our homework? You.

KIQUI: You know us because you gave us your time.

ALBERTO: You're cool, Mom.

KIQUI: Don't you understand? It's thanks to you we *have* a family. I miss everybody, I really do. There are days when I need to be with you.

> *Granny-Granma, leaning on the handrail, whimpers loudly.*

MAMA RITA: Ma, stop clowning around. You're going to fall.

GRAN: I want to go home! You threw me out.

MAMA RITA: Come down from there.

GRAN: I can't Rita. My feet went to sleep.

MAMA RITA: Go get her, Alberto.

> *Alberto begrudgingly goes to get Granny-Granma. He picks her up and carries her to the living room. He seats her in an armchair. Granny-Granma smiles to an absent audience.*

MAMA RITA: Now I want everyone to calm down.

KIQUI: Sure, Mom. But you don't know what it's like to have a castrating father.

> *Granny-Granma emits a malicious laugh.*

MAMA RITA: OK, this discussion has ended.

> *Mama Rita gets up and goes to the dining room table. She gathers the rest of the dirty dishes. She carries them to the kitchen. While she does this she sings to herself, "Voy a apagar la luz," by Manzanero.*
>
> *Alberto gets up and goes up the stairs. He exits. Granny-Granma starts to pray.*

KIQUI: *(In a confidential tone)* I can tell she's suffering.
SILVIA: It's natural.
KIQUI: The only one I really fell for was a guy named Alberto.
GONZALO: We need to talk to Dad.
KIQUI: This guy Alberto fascinated me.
GONZALO: Silvia, you were the worst.
SILVIA: The worst? How?
GONZALO: You didn't support Mama Rita.
SILVIA: I did support her.
KIQUI: I don't know why you're on Dad's side.
GRAN: *(Praying)* And this one is for my daughter Rita, please help her through this moment. Our father who art in heaven. . .
SILVIA: I'm not on anyone's side.
GONZALO: Tomorrow I'm going to go to Dad's office.
KIQUI: He's a ridiculous old man.
SILVIA: Don't be offensive.
KIQUI: What are you, a hippie or what? Love and peace.
SILVIA: Your frame of reference is very narrow.
GRAN: This one is for my grandchildren, Gonzalo, Kiqui, Silvia and Alberto, please protect them from all ill. Our father who art in heaven. . .

> *Mama Rita comes in from the kitchen.*
> *She carries a tray with cake and plates*
> *to the coffee table.*

GRAN: Is that the wine cake?

MAMA RITA: *(Placing the tray on the table)* We forgot the cake. Eat it. I'm on a diet starting today. *(She exits through the kitchen door.)*

KIQUI: *(Getting ready to cut the cake)* Who wants cake?

GRAN: *(Enthusiastically)* I do, dear.

GONZALO: Everyone.

> *Kiqui distributes the plates with*
> *pieces of cake. She gives Granny-*
> *Granma a much larger piece, compared*
> *to the others. They eat in silence.*

KIQUI: And you all never realized what was happening?

GONZALO: Mmh, it's delicious. Go get some napkins, Silvia.

SILVIA: You get up and get them.

GONZALO: They hid it from us.

SILVIA: Are you deaf?

GONZALO: It's delicious, but a little dry. The other day I noticed Mama Rita was acting a little strange, but this kind of a tragedy never entered my mind. . .

KIQUI: Do you know the woman?

GONZALO: No.

KIQUI: Didn't you say she was Dad's secretary?

GONZALO: That's what Alberto says, but I don't believe it.

KIQUI: What's she like?

SILVIA: I don't know her. I've just talked to her on the phone.

KIQUI: Does she have a young-sounding voice?

SILVIA: I think so. She's got a high voice, sort of shrill.

KIQUI: That type is terrible. They never miss a trick.

GRAN: They get whoever they want.

KIQUI: Mama Rita must be feeling awful. Humiliated.

SILVIA: Devalued. We have to keep telling her how good and how young she looks.

KIQUI: I hate to even think about what's ahead. Imagine her alone, devalued and without a man. She's gonna want us to go everywhere with her.

SILVIA: To supply the affection she'll be missing.

GONZALO: *(To Kiqui)* You'll be safe.

KIQUI: Don't be so sure. I can just see her calling Venezuela long distance to tell me her troubles.

GONZALO: We'll be the real losers in all of this.

GRAN: This prayer is to help my daughter Rita's marriage. Our father who art in heaven. . .

> *Mama Rita comes out of the kitchen and climbs the stairs. They all look at her attentively. She exits.*

SILVIA: I'll bet she's gone to her bedroom to cry.

KIQUI: I'll go console her.

SILVIA: You're crazy. Let her get it off her chest. Crying is beneficial.

KIQUI: That's true. I have an acting teacher who makes us practice crying. And it really does act as a therapy for me. Well, in the theater it's used for. . . well, I don't really understand, it's a very modern technique. . .

> *Alberto comes down the stairs. He goes to the living room. He cuts a piece of cake. He places it on a plate. He sits down.*

GONZALO: Let's see those red eyes.

KIQUI: Leave him alone, Gonzalo.

GONZALO: Smoking pot makes you hungry.

ALBERTO: You're just like Dad. You make me sick.

KIQUI: And Mom?

ALBERTO: She shut herself up in her room.

KIQUI: I'm going to go up.

GONZALO: Don't be a jerk. We already told you not to.

GRAN: This last prayer is for Margarita, the lame one. Our father who art in heaven. . .

ALBERTO: This cake is horrible.

GONZALO: Alberto's the one who's gonna have to take care of Mom.

ALBERTO: You're crazy.

SILVIA: Granny-Granma can take care of her.

GRAN: I've lost my strength, dear. Anyway, Rita is very independent and hard to deal with.

SILVIA: It was a joke.

GRAN: I want more cake, Silvia.

KIQUI: Why doesn't someone turn the TV on?

> *Silvia gets up and cuts another piece of cake for Granny-Granma.*

ALBERTO: Do you want to see the "Girls of the Mississippi"?

GONZALO: I've already seen that piece of porno.

KIQUI: I haven't.

GRAN: Your mother will come down and she'll get mad.

ALBERTO: She's already seen it twice.

GRAN: Oh, OK.

ALBERTO: I'll go get it. I think it's in my room.

> *He climbs the stairs and exits.*

GONZALO: Let's open Dad's cognac.

SILVIA: He'll get mad.

GONZALO: Whoever abandons his house loses everything. Don't you know that rule?

KIQUI: How would she know?

SILVIA: You all are the experts. I'm not promiscuous.

KIQUI: Ha!

SILVIA: Laugh as much as you want.

GRAN: Can I tell you all something? But don't tell Rita I told you.

> *Gonzalo goes to the bar and opens a bottle of cognac. He pours himself a glass.*

KIQUI: *(Enjoying herself)* Don't worry, Gran, we won't tell Mom
that you told us not to tell her what you're going to tell us.

GRAN: I think Rita's been acting very strange. She's sort of
distracted. This morning when she was preparing dinner, she
couldn't find the sugar and you know where she had put it? In
the refrigerator.

KIQUI: *(To Gonzalo)* Did I tell you how I flipped out once for a guy?
In Venezuela. He was a beautiful Mathematical Physicist. It
was love at first sight, I tell you. They used to call him
"superman." You can imagine how handsome he was. But I
held back--he was married. His wife was a meatball with legs.
A real retard. But I didn't feel like going for it. . .

> *Alberto enters. He comes down the
> stairs with the video tape.*

GONZALO: *(To Kiqui)* Right now I'm going out with a really pretty
girl. She's only nineteen. She's beautiful.

KIQUI: That's good. Maybe now you'll leave Maria Elena alone.

GONZALO: Hm.

ALBERTO: *(With the videotape in his hand)* Do you want to watch
it?

KIQUI: Just the beginning, so I can see if I've already seen it.

SILVIA: Those movies are all the same.

ALBERTO: Are you going to watch it, Granny-Granma?

GRAN: Go ahead and put it on. I'll close my eyes. I'm busy praying
anyway. When I pray I generally close my eyes.

> *Alberto goes to the TV and puts the
> tape in the VCR. Gonzalo discreetly gets
> up and goes to the dining room table. He
> carries with him the bottle of cognac, his
> glass and the newspaper. He sits down and
> turns to the paper. He drinks.*

GONZALO: Leave the sound off. Mama Rita might not like it.

> *A pornographic movie comes on the
> screen. Alberto goes to the dining room
> table and sits down. Kiqui and Silvia*

> *look at the screen with an indifferent
> attitude. Granny-Granma opens and
> closes her eyes frequently. She is
> curious.*

GRAN: I already told you all about Margarita, didn't I?

> *Silence.*

GRAN: Well, it turns out that the other day they found her lying on the floor. Naked and wet. Then they realized she was dead. Just think about an end like that. Dead in the bathroom. They brought her out and I think they covered her with some rags. Or with her own clothes. But what were her own clothes anyway? Old rags, that's all. So we all found out Margarita was dead. . .

ALBERTO: Is that blonde on now, the one with the ribbon in her hair?

KIQUI: Yeah.

GONZALO: Hm.

GRAN: Everybody knew her and even though she was so hard to get along with--remember?--everybody loved her. Can you imagine? Every single vendor in the market contributed something toward her coffin. That's what I call luck. You can die and not even a rooster will crow. Yeah, you can kick the bucket and it might be that nobody even notices. And since I'm living alone, well, you know, any minute. . .

SILVIA: Those actors must make a fortune, don't you think?

KIQUI: That blonde is terrible.

ALBERTO: Wait til the Oriental one comes on. She's a looker.

SILVIA: The guy's the good-looking one.

GRAN: So, they had the wake and all that. Bertha, my neighbor, was the one who told me everything. She said everybody went to the funeral. They must have really loved her, don't you think? But you never would have guessed it. I always thought nobody even noticed her. So many years wandering the streets nobody paid any attention anymore. But they're not the forgotten ones. We're the forgotten ones. Not that I would speak badly of your mother. Rita's always taken care of me, but she's married. A married woman has her problems. You see, now your father is running around like a dirty old man after another woman. That's the last straw. I understand Rita, but sometimes I miss her. Really. I miss you all, too. And don't think I'm just saying that. You're my only grandchildren. . .

> *Kiqui yawns.*

GRAN: Margarita was a little devil, but she always waited on us. She was very helpful. Of course we would give her a tip. But, what do you think she would spend her money on? Wine. She was a real wine-o. When I get to heaven, the Lord is going to ask me--what bad things did you do during your life? Did you smoke? Drink? And I'll say no. So they'll send me to hell for being so stupid! *(She laughs.)* But Margarita, she'll be in heaven, right next to the angels. . .

> *The telephone rings. They all get tense. Kiqui gets up from her seat and moves decisively to answer it.*

KIQUI: *(Into the phone)* Hello. Yes. Who's calling? Oh, yes. I'll get her. *(Goes to the stairway.)* Mom! Telephone!
MAMA RITA'S VOICE: I'm coming!
KIQUI: It's Jose Francisco.

> *Everyone tries to hide their expectation.*

KIQUI: It's Jose Francisco.

> *Mama Rita appears and hurriedly comes down the stairway. She reaches the phone and answers. She is dressed to go out, looks very made up.*

MAMA RITA: *(Into the phone)* Yes, yes. No, dear. That's fine. Bye.

> *Mama Rita hangs up. She laughs nervously. She doesn't move for a*

*moment, as she looks at each one of
them. There is a long silence.*

MAMA RITA: I have a surprise for you. Some good news.

GRAN: Oh, no.

MAMA RITA: Well, I hope that. .. I have to tell you. . . I've met a
man. I'm going to get married again. I hope you understand.
You too, Ma.

KIQUI: What else?

GONZALO: But what's the matter with you two? Have you and Dad
gone crazy? You just break up a family in a matter of seconds.

MAMA RITA: Thirty-five years of marriage isn't a matter of
seconds.

GONZALO: That's all the more reason. . .

MAMA RITA: You're all responsible adults now. . .

GONZALO: Does Alberto seem responsible to you? Who's he gonna
live with?

SILVIA: A family break-up of this kind can cause. . .

MAMA RITA: Albertito can do what he wants. . .

ALBERTO: Mom, everything I do bothers you. The fact is you want
to get rid of me. I'm in the way.

GRAN: Me, too, I'm in the way, too.

SILVIA: I can't believe you don't want to take care of Granny-
Granma. Your own mother.

GONZALO: Mom, you can't be this irresponsible.

MAMA RITA: Don't be so selfish.

KIQUI: I'll have to be a mother to my brothers!

ALBERTO: Cut it out!

GONZALO: So who is this guy?

MAMA RITA: He's an anthropologist and, well, he wants to meet
all of you. He's a very responsible man. And he loves me.

SILVIA: Hmm.

MAMA RITA: You're all grown now. I raised you.

GONZALO: Yeah, you gave us Coca Cola and cold tamales to eat.

KIQUI: That's something I'll never forget.

SILVIA: And when you knitted sweaters for us they were always too
big or too small. Never the right size.

GONZALO: And when at the beginning of every school year you made paper covers for my books, you did it with so little love that I was crushed.

KIQUI: How about when you used to pull my hair because I didn't know the multiplication tables?

SILVIA: No sense of pedagogy.

KIQUI: You never wanted to play with us. We were just children.

GONZALO: And every day of my childhood I had to listen to you bitch about cooking.

ALBERTO: And since you don't like cooking, your chilaquiles come out sweet.

KIQUI: You never used to let me go anywhere with my friends. That's why I ran away from home.

ALBERTO: Poor Dad.

GRAN: There are no divorces in my family!

GONZALO: She's right. We're going to be the scandal of the family.

GRAN: I never did this to your father, Rita.

MAMA RITA: You shut up, you're my enemy.

KIQUI: She's your mother, Mom. Don't talk to her like that.

ALBERTO: You owe her some respect.

GRAN: Raise crows and they'll poke your eyes out.

MAMA RITA: I have the right to remake my life. The same as you do, Gonzalo.

GONZALO: It's not the same. Don't try to justify your actions. How can you deceive Dad like this? What does this man think of you?

KIQUI: I'll bet he doesn't take you seriously. A fifty-year old woman who abandons her family because of an affair.

MAMA RITA: It's more than an affair, Kiqui.

GONZALO: That's even worse. I can't tell my friends about this.

MAMA RITA: You'd prefer that I be the abandoned woman.

ALBERTO: We just don't want you to leave Dad. He's always been a man who's more or less kept up his end of the bargain.

MAMA RITA: What about me?

SILVIA: You've only half kept yours.

GRAN: It's all my fault. I never taught her how to take care of a husband. It's my fault, kids.

KIQUI: No, Granny-Granma, that's not it. The serious part is that she's abandoning her home.

ALBERTO: And she's leaving me.

GONZALO: This boy's a pothead and a flake.

SILVIA: That's right, Alberto is very confused.

ALBERTO: You're more confused. You're crazy. You act like a spaced-out nun.

KIQUI: And look at Gonzalo, your so-called love. I think you've made him impotent. Poor thing, he's not happy.

GONZALO: What about you? Nymphomaniac!

GRAN: I already told you your grandfather was impotent on our honeymoon. But I didn't leave him. I can just imagine what would have happened to me if I had.

GONZALO: I'll bet Dad feels totally humiliated.

SILVIA: That would explain his actions with Magali.

GRAN: Poor girl, she'll never be happy with your father.

MAMA RITA: OK, Ma, now you <u>are</u> leaving!

> *Granny-Granma shrieks with pain.*
> *She falls to the floor. Gonzalo picks*
> *her up. He takes her pulse. Mama*
> *Rita goes toward her.*

MAMA RITA: *(Worried)* Mother! Mother! What's the matter? What is it, Gonzalo?

GONZALO: *(Staring at her)* Nothing. Just nerves.

GRAN: I'm sick of your saying there's nothing wrong with me. I don't know how you can call yourself a doctor, you don't know anything.

MAMA RITA: OK, Ma, calm down.

GRAN: Nobody loves me.

MAMA RITA: Do you want a cup of tea?

GRAN: No, you Jezebel!

GONZALO: We have to talk about dividing the possessions. I don't want this jerk to get anything of my Dad's.

KIQUI: I guess Gonzalez Marquez is right for the case. He's a good friend of Dad's.

GONZALO: It's a shame that a friend of the family has to know about Mom's problems.

GRAN: Never hang your dirty laundry in public.

KIQUI: You're funny, Mom. Your life is like a musical comedy. You want everyone to dance to the music of your play.

GRAN: Gonzalito, why does it hurt right here? *(She points to her stomach.)*

GONZALO: I'll bet Dad doesn't want to see us, not because he's afraid to, but because he's ashamed.

GRAN: Gonzalito. . .

MAMA RITA: I see now that one's good intentions are worthless.

SILVIA: These family problems are very serious. They can seriously scar each one of the members.

MAMA RITA: What do you want me to do?

KIQUI: We want you to stay with your family. At your age it's hard to start over.

GONZALO: For your own good.

GRAN: Better the devil you know than the one you don't know.

MAMA RITA: But nothing's going to change. You all are my children. I'll never leave you.

GONZALO: Stay, Mama Rita.

KIQUI: Yes, stay.

SILVIA: Stay.

ALBERTO: Stay.

GRAN: Yes, Ritita, stay.

GONZALO: We all love you very much.

KIQUI: We want the best for you.

MAMA RITA: *(Sighing deeply)* How can I say no. . ?

> From the street we hear the sound of a horn being blown insistently. Mama Rita smiles and looks at each one of them. Her hands fall in an attitude of one who is conquered. They all smile, pleased. Mama Rita takes off her coat and everyone notices her low-cut blouse. She gives each a kiss. They all answer: "Thanks, Mommy." Then she turns around and goes toward the door that leads to the street.

MAMA RITA: Arriva derchi, children. *(She exits.)*

KIQUI: *(Resigned)* I'll send you a postcard.

GONZALO: *(Same)* I'll come by for dinner.
SILVIA: *(Same)* I'll call tomorrow.
ALBERTO: *(Same)* I won't come in too late tonight.
GRAN: *(Same)* I'll wait to have dinner with you. . . Well, like I was
saying, what Bertha told me is amazing. Everyone was at the
funeral. Praying. Everybody from the market came and what
do you think happened? They were praying and praying and
praying; then they realized that Margarita was moving an arm
slowly. Very slowly, up to her head. I imagine her head was
shaved. And they were so shocked they all ran out of the
funeral shouting and, of course, she wasn't dead. She was
alive. That's right. Margarita came back to life.

> *Kiqui goes to the television and turns it
> off.*

THE END

Víctor Hugo Rascón Banda was born in a very small mining town in the state of Chihuahua in 1948. He came to the capital to study law in 1974, obtaining his Ph.D. in 1979, the year in which he also began to write for the theater. Though he has divided his time between his two professions throughout his career, he has produced an impressive body of works and has become a prominent figure in the arts and one of the foremost representatives of what has been dubbed "la nueva dramaturgia," the generation of playwrights which took up the torch after the Carballido/Magaña/Hernández generation. His works include about fifteen plays and several screenplays; three of his plays have been translated into English for bilingual productions for very receptive Mexican-American audiences in the United States. During the last decade his plays have frequently been chosen to represent Mexico at international festivals; he has recently been anthologized in a collection of Mexican plays edited in Germany, and in the volume on Mexico of the elaborate collection of Spanish and Latin American plays published by the Fondo de Cultura Económica.

As one of the core members of Vicente Leñero's ongoing dramatic writing workshop, Rascón experimented with hyperrealism and produced a number of plays which fall under this rubric. *Blue Beach (Playa azul)*, however, written in 1982, published in 1986, and staged in 1989 by Raúl Quintanilla, falls into another category of the realisms of Rascón Banda, "poetic realism," perhaps the most original of all of the styles with which the author has experimented. Though realistic in most ways, this play employs the unreal and the surreal to create the atmosphere of putrefaction, of phantasm, and of decadence which makes it so memorable. Ambition and corruption have led to the disintegration of a family and the downfall of its patriarch: the natural world (seagulls, coconuts, breezes) reflects the inner state of the characters.

After *Contrabando* (another one of his poetic realistic plays), *Blue Beach* is the play with which Rascón is most satisfied. It is very representative of his work and will give the reader a good sense of the capabilities of this playwright, as well as the nature of his concerns and the originality of his style.

BLUE BEACH

by Víctor Hugo Rascón Banda

CHARACTERS:

SERGIO, 25 years old
MATIAS, 70 years old
TERESA, 40 years old
SILVIA, 28 years old
MOTHER, 52 years old
GARZA: 55 years old

SET:

The play takes place during the present time at a hotel on the coast of Michoacán, Mexico. It has been constructed on a solitary site, far from any human settlement.

Lobby of an old hotel, almost in ruins. Left, rear, the front desk and a hallway which leads to the rooms on the first floor. To the right is a wooden stairway that leads to the restaurant; it is missing several steps and the handrail is broken. Another ladder, larger and more solid, leads to the upstairs rooms. To one side of this stairway are a few steps leading down to the maids' quarters. To the rear of the stage, which is the area of the swimming pool, is a magnolia tree, several old, neglected palm trees and the thatched roofs of the rustic beach umbrellas. Behind the latter is the sea, which we can sense and hear. A short flight of stairs near the front desk leads to the hotel parking lot and to the highway. A rotating ceiling fan hangs from the ceiling. The following handwritten signs are hung in different places: "THE RESTAURANT IS CLOSED," "THE SHOWERS ONLY HAVE WATER FROM 8 A.M. TO 10 A.M. AND FROM 8 P.M. TO 10 P.M.," "CHECK-OUT TIME IS 12:00," " LEAVE ALL VALUABLES AT THE FRONT DESK," "SWIMMING POOL CLOSED." "Blue Beach" is written on the rubber welcome mats near the exits to the parking lot and the swimming pool. In the lobby there is furniture made of wood, wicker and leather, all from the Pacific coast area; it is in poor condition. On a thick pillar located next to the swimming pool hangs a large portrait of a General .

I

> *It is midnight. The place is empty. The sound of waves breaking nearby is heard. A dog barks several times. Sergio appears on the stairs which lead to the highway. He is wearing modern clothing, of good quality. He carries a sports bag on his shoulder. He looks emaciated, as if he had been sick. He looks the place over, checking out the swimming pool, the restaurant and the hallway. He approaches the front desk and bangs on it with his hand. He discovers a bell and rings it repeatedly. He looks for the keys to the rooms behind the desk but doesn't find them. He tries to open the cash register but is unsuccessful. He goes into the hallway and tries to open two rooms, without success. He returns to the front desk, rings the bell and kicks the counter. He sits down in an armchair and waits. He leans back. He closes his eyes. We hear footsteps approaching; from the hallway comes Matias, who comes to him and touches him.*

MATIAS: Get out of here.
SERGIO: Where were you?
MATIAS: If you don't leave, I'm calling the police.
SERGIO: Are you crazy? What you should be doing is looking after all this. You shouldn't leave the front desk unattended.

MATIAS: I'm not responsible for what'll happen if you don't get out of here.

SERGIO: Shut your trap and get a room ready for me. I'm very tired.

MATIAS: Do you think I can't throw you out? You just wait and see. *(He goes behind the counter and brings out a pistol.)* Scram.

SERGIO: Put that down. Don't be a fool. Don't you know who I am?

MATIAS: I don't know and I don't care.

SERGIO: I'm Garza's son.

MATIAS: Mr. Garza doesn't have any sons. They all died a long time ago.

SERGIO: So who am I? Do what I say or tomorrow you'll be out of a job. Do you hear me?

> *Matias hesitates. He tucks the pistol into his belt.*

MATIAS: I could kill you if I wanted.

SERGIO: Go get a room ready for me.

MATIAS: There aren't any.

SERGIO: They're all full?

MATIAS: No.

SERGIO: So?

MATIAS: They were damaged in the earthquake.

SERGIO: *(Looking toward the hallway)* What about those? Give me the keys.

MATIAS: Teresa has them.

SERGIO: Call her.

MATIAS: She's not here.

SERGIO: Well she should be. That's what she gets paid for. Where did she go?

MATIAS: She went into the ocean. And she's not coming back. She was drunk, she was singing. She climbed into a boat with no oars.

SERGIO: Bring me a blanket and a pillow.

MATIAS: I don't have any.

SERGIO: Shit, man. You're worthless.

> *Matias doesn't move. Sergio stretches out in the armchair.*

MATIAS: That's where I sleep.
SERGIO: Where you used to sleep. Go away and leave me alone.
MATIAS: That's my chair.
SERGIO: It used to be.

> *Sergio turns his back to him. Matias comes*
> *over to him and throws him to the ground.*
> *Sergio gets up.*

SERGIO: That does it, you old goat. *(He throws himself on Matias*
to beat him. Matias takes the pistol out. They fight. Sergio
takes the pistol away from him and hits him over the head with
it.) You old fool.

> *Enter Teresa, returning from the market. She*
> *dresses like a man. She is an ugly, robust*
> *woman. She tries to pull them apart.*

TERESA: Leave him alone! Let him go!

> *Sergio and Matias separate.*

SERGIO: Good thing you showed up. I was about to let this old man
have it.
TERESA: How can you treat an old man like that? (She goes to
Matias and examines his head.) Let me see.
MATIAS: I'm OK.
TERESA: Yeah, sure. Just look what he did to you.
MATIAS: I said I'm fine.
TERESA: He cracked your skull open. I'll fix it. You're bleeding.
MATIAS: That's not my blood. That's the blood of the people killed
in the earthquake.
TERESA: Go wash and come right back.
MATIAS: They splashed their blood on me. It stuck to me and I
haven't been able to wash it off even with ocean water.
SERGIO: What's he talking about?
TERESA: You heard him.
SERGIO: He's crazy.
TERESA: I'll put alcohol and methiolate on it, but you have to wash
it first. Go get some water.
MATIAS: I have a lot to do before I go to bed.
TERESA: You can do it later.

MATIAS: I have to lock all the doors and the windows. I have to pick up the coconuts and cut the magnolia flowers like you told me. I have to make a broom and. . .

TERESA: I'll do it all. I'll fix you up and you'll go to sleep.

MATIAS: (Laughing) Sleep? Who told you I sleep? (He laughs.) Sleep. . . I don't even close my eyes. I watch over this day and night. And I fight off the mosquitoes. If I fall asleep, they'll eat me alive.

TERESA: OK. Do whatever you want. Just don't come crying to me when your scalp is covered in worms. Have you already forgotten those ticks I dug out of your ears the other day?

SERGIO: I'm very tired. Give me the key to the room off the terrace.

Teresa takes a key ring from her bosom and gives a key to Matias.

TERESA: Get number 207 ready.

MATIAS: Not that one, Teresa.

SERGIO: I want the one off the terrace.

TERESA: Get 207 ready and stock it with everything.

SERGIO: Can't I even choose the one I want?

TERESA: Yes, when it's possible.

MATIAS: Not that one, Teresa. Remember the man we found in there.

SERGIO: What man?

TERESA: He dreamed there was a dead man in there.

MATIAS: He'd been dead a few days and he had a syringe in his hand. There were flies and worms. It was an ugly dream.

TERESA: And it wasn't in that room. It was in the one off the terrace. So get going.

MATIAS: There's no paper in there.

TERESA: Take him a box of Kleenex from my room.

MATIAS: He'll have to have remade soap. There's none of the other left.

SERGIO: What's that?

TERESA: It's soap that he makes, from the left over pieces from the whole year.

SERGIO: And he's going to give me that shit?

TERESA: It'll have to do. Here we only have two kinds of soap: reconstituted and Palmolive. And the Palmolive's all gone. *(Matias leaves.)*

SERGIO: How is it possible that you keep that old guy on here?

TERESA: I didn't bring him here. Talk to your father. Matias was here before I got here. Aren't you ashamed you hit him?

SERGIO: He's dangerous. I'm going to fire him tomorrow.

TERESA: Did you hire him? The only people that can fire him are your father and me. How did you get here?

SERGIO: How do you think?

TERESA: Couldn't you have let me know? I would have picked you up.

SERGIO: I tried to call, but the operator told me the phone had been disconnected.

TERESA: It went bad with the earthquake.

SERGIO: Why are you lying? It was because you didn't pay the bill.

TERESA: So what are you doing here? Don't tell me you've come to spend a vacation. You've never even stopped in before.

SERGIO: My father asked me to come.

TERESA: Oh, yeah?

SERGIO: Don't tell me you didn't know.

TERESA: I didn't know about you.

SERGIO: Is he awake? I'd like to see him.

TERESA: Wait til tomorrow.

SERGIO: And mother? Did she come with him?

TERESA: She got here yesterday.

SERGIO: How is she?

TERESA: What do you mean?

SERGIO: Her health.

TERESA: Who knows. She seems fine. Bossy as ever.

SERGIO: *(Opening his bag)* With all the excitement, I almost forgot. I brought you a bottle. Guess what it is.

TERESA: I don't like riddles.

SERGIO: Remember what you always used to drink at home? Chinguere, the one you like.

TERESA: Thanks. I can't believe you remembered. You can't get this here, not even for medicinal purposes.

SERGIO: Why don't you have some?

TERESA: Later. When your sister gets here. We'll celebrate. I've been waiting for her for three days.

SERGIO: I'm glad she's coming. I'm dying to see her.

TERESA: Your father sent for her.

SERGIO: Why?

TERESA: You'll find out soon enough. I'm no gossip.

SERGIO: Aren't you going to offer me anything to eat?

TERESA: The restaurant is closed.

SERGIO: Surely there's still someone in the kitchen.

TERESA: Didn't you read the sign?

SERGIO: Loan me the key.

TERESA: What for?

SERGIO: I'll find something. I know how to cook.

TERESA: The cupboards are empty. We haven't sold food here in a long time.

SERGIO: What? Why not?

TERESA: Because there's no money to buy it with, and no one to cook it, and no one to serve it.

SERGIO: What about you?

TERESA: I'm not a cook or a maid or a waitress.

SERGIO: From the looks of things you've ruined this hotel.

TERESA: You've got it backwards. This hotel has ruined me.

SERGIO: I can hardly believe it. It's unrecognizable. I never thought I'd find it like this.

TERESA: It might be unrecognizable for you, since you've never stepped foot on it, but for me and Matias it's very recognizable.

SERGIO: You've frightened all the tourists away.

TERESA: Am I that ugly?

SERGIO: You've managed to run them off.

TERESA: You think so?

SERGIO: You admit it.

TERESA: I admit nothing.

SERGIO: My father should make you account for all this.

TERESA: Oh, yeah? Really?

SERGIO: You sucked it dry.

TERESA: You all sucked it dry, kiddo. Where do you think all the money came from to help your sister in Mexico City and to pay for your mother's trips and to send to you? Where did it come from, huh?

SERGIO: My father had enough money to support us without needing a dime from this miserable hotel.

TERESA: He used to have. A long long time ago. How much property does he own now? How much money does he have in the bank? How many businesses? Huh?

SERGIO: *(Looking the room over)* You let this place go to hell. . . it's gone to hell.

TERESA: We let it, kiddo, we let it. . . *(A dog can be heard barking.)* Sounds like someone's here. *(The two of them remain in an expectant attitude.)*

*Silvia enters. She is an attractive woman,
fashionably dressed. She is carrying a small
suitcase.*

SILVIA: Teresa, you shithead. Why didn't you meet me?

TERESA: Hey, don't blame me. I've gone to the port three days in a row. After three I give up. Couldn't you have been more specific about the day you were coming?

SILVIA: Now you'll have to pay the cab I took.

TERESA: Sure thing. You can always count on your cashier here to pick up all the tabs.

SERGIO: Aren't you going to speak to me? You two can fight later.

SILVIA: *(Coldly)* I didn't expect to find you here.

SERGIO: Neither did I.

SILVIA: *(To Teresa)* Didn't you tell me they hadn't called him?

TERESA: He just blew in out of nowhere, a few minutes ago.

SERGIO: I don't need an invitation. This is mine too, isn't it?

TERESA: Who'd you leave your little girl with?

SILVIA: I gave her away.

TERESA: Why didn't you tell me you were going to do that? I have a huge maternal heart. She would have been very happy with me.

SILVIA: Well, you adopt her, then. We'll see how long you can stand her. She's a real nuisance and very demanding.

TERESA: Just like her mother.

SILVIA: She'd love to be like me. But she's as horrible as her father.

TERESA: If he's so ugly, why'd you let him make the girl?

SILVIA: I was an idiot. Back then. Ooh, my feet are killing me.

TERESA: Take your boots off. You'll fry in them here.

SILVIA: Help me.

*Silvia sits down and stretches her legs out.
Teresa kneels down and pulls at her boots.*

TERESA: You should wear boots your own size instead of forcing these little ones on. You just want your feet to look small.

SILVIA: *(Rubbing her feet)* Ahh, that feels better. . . Where's Dad?

TERESA: He hasn't come out of his room. You'll see him tomorrow.

SILVIA: And Matias? He usually comes running when I get here.

TERESA: You almost didn't find him alive. If I hadn't walked in, your brother would have killed him.

SILVIA: He'll take advantage of anyone.

SERGIO: You don't even know what happened, so keep your opinions to yourself.

TERESA: I'll bring out some glasses so we can toast to the travelers.

SILVIA: Where am I going to sleep?

TERESA: Give me your bag. I'll put it in my room. It's the coolest. I fixed you a bed there.

> *Teresa goes toward the maids' quarters and enters one of the rooms.*

SERGIO: So what's new in Mexico?

SILVIA: Everything's the same. *(Pause.)* How about you? Where've you been roaming?

SERGIO: Here and there. I'm OK.

SILVIA: Good.

SERGIO: You still at the same job?

SILVIA: No. Now I'm with an American company. Are you well now?

SERGIO: Completely.

SILVIA: Good. Did they release you?

SERGIO: Yep.

SILVIA: You'll be at it again in no time.

SERGIO: Are you gonna start in on me?

SILVIA: It's not my fault.

SERGIO: Look, Silvia, I'm serious. You may not believe me, but I've changed.

SILVIA: You look the same to me.

SERGIO: Cut the kidding. I've changed. I've thought it all out. Lots of things have happened. I can't even begin to tell you. I'm sorry about what I did to you, really. I'll pay it all back some day. The money, that is. The rest, I know I can't make up for it, but I swear I'm different now. You don't believe me, do you?

SILVIA: No.

SERGIO: That's OK. It'll take a little time. You're gonna see how serious I am.

SILVIA: Do what you want. You don't have to convince me of anything. Unless you're planning on asking me for something.

SERGIO: The only thing I want from you is for you to believe me when I say from here on out it's gonna be different.

SILVIA: Would you believe I couldn't care less? Just don't come near my place or cross my path, and I'll be happy.

SERGIO: Fine. I deserve it.

> *Matias enters and is happy to see Silvia.*

MATIAS: Silvia, good to see you. *(Silvia gets up and hugs him.)* I'm glad you're here. I've been cooling some coconuts for you. Should I bring them out? You'll want a cool drink.

SILVIA: Later. How have you been?

MATIAS: Fine, fine. I got the vitamins you sent, but I'm out now. Did you bring any more?

SILVIA: Yes, but different ones. These have cod liver oil in them.

MATIAS: Really? Just what I need.

SILVIA: And I brought you a radio, so you can hear El Canonazo. Teresa said you missed your show.

MATIAS: It's true. My radio quit working the day of the earthquake. But it saved my life. Instead of falling on me, the roof fell on the radio and it kept playing for quite a while. I tried all night to get it out from under the rubble--I could hear where the music was coming from--but the next day, when I finally got to it, it was dead. I threw it into the sea so it can play with the mermaids. *(He laughs.)*

SILVIA: Well now you have a new radio so you can hear your Hurricanes from Michoacan sing.

MATIAS: Have you heard "The Storm"? How about "The Dust on These Roads"?

SILVIA: I think so, but I'm not sure.

> *Teresa comes out of her room with a tray and*
> *glasses. Matias goes to help her.*

SERGIO: Why do you pay attention to him? What's the point of encouraging his craziness?

SILVIA: Who say he's crazy?

SERGIO: Didn't you hear him? But this is his last night to sleep here. I'm planning to fire him.

SILVIA: What right do you have?

> *Teresa opens the bottle, pours the drinks and*
> *offers one to Sergio.*

SERGIO: None for me, thanks.

TERESA: What's this?

SERGIO: I don't drink anymore. Bring me instead one of those coconuts that the old man prepared for Silvia.

TERESA: *(To Matias)* Here's one for you.

MATIAS: Not now. I'm about to start taking vitamins and they won't have any effect if I drink.

TERESA: My gain. My bottle will last longer this way. Cheers, Silviana.

SILVIA: Cheers, Terruca. *(They both drink and refill their glasses.)*

TERESA: *(To Matias)* Bring Sergio a cold coconut.

Matias leaves.

SERGIO: *(To Silvia)* Look what Teresa has done to this place. It looks like a jail with those signs. *(To Teresa)* Didn't it even occur to you to sweep? What good is the old man? I can't believe there aren't any tourists or any money to fix this place up.

TERESA: It's one and the same thing: There aren't any tourists, there isn't any money. There isn't any money, so there aren't any tourists. It's that easy.

SERGIO: It looks like a ghost house or the ruins after a bombing.

TERESA: If you only knew, kiddo. And you'll find out soon enough. Cheers, Silviana.

SILVIA: Cheers, Terruca.

Matias enters carrying a prepared coconut.

SERGIO: No straw?

MATIAS: We're out.

TERESA: He can get you a glass.

SERGIO: I don't dare even ask. He'll say they all broke. *(He lifts the coconut to his mouth and takes a long sip which he later spits out with revulsion.)* Crazy bastard. What's in this?

MATIAS: All I did was take off the top and make the hole.

SERGIO: Taste this, Teresa. *(He hands her the coconut.)*

TERESA: *(Tasting it)* It's fine. I don't taste anything bad. You try it, Silvia. *(She hands her the coconut.)*

SILVIA: *(Tasting it)* Delicious. *(To Matias)* It was already written that this one was for me.

SERGIO: So the one with the bitter mouth is me, huh?

MATIAS: Do you want me to prepare you another one?

SERGIO: Of course not. Do you think I want to die by poisoning?

TERESA: Have a drink with us.

SERGIO: I already told you I don't drink. I'm going to bed. You two
  will want to be alone; you probably have a lot to talk about.
TERESA: *(To Matias)* Show him his room.
SERGIO: I'll go alone. He might strangle me on the way. *(To
  Matias)* Give me the key. *(Matias gives it to him.)* And the
  pistol.
MATIAS: *(To Teresa)* Should I?
TERESA: Give it to him. He's in charge of this hotel from now on.

Matias hands the pistol over to him.

SERGIO: See you tomorrow.
TERESA: Sleep well.

Sergio exits. Matias starts toward the swimming pool.

TERESA: What are you going to do?
MATIAS: I'm going to cut the magnolias.
TERESA: It's awfully dark. Don't fall. The ladder's old.
MATIAS: Old for the old. *(He exits.)*
SILVIA: How've you been? You've gained weight.
TERESA: What do you expect? With this good life. You, on the
  other hand, look like you never eat. You'll blow away.
SILVIA: I haven't been so well lately. I've been under a lot of stress.
TERESA: You suffer because you want to. Why don't you come
  here?
SILVIA: I'd die from boredom. *(Pause.)* What's going on, Teresa?
TERESA: Nothing. Don't worry.
SILVIA: Do you know why he called us?
TERESA: No.
SILVIA: Why all the mystery?
TERESA: The only thing I know is that we're all going to hell in a
  hand basket.
SILVIA: Why?
TERESA: It's finally all over.
SILVIA: What is?
TERESA: You live in Mexico City and don't read the papers? And I
  guess you don't get to Morelia very often anymore?
SILVIA: I don't have time for anything.
TERESA: You don't watch television? Listen to the radio? It's been
  on all the news programs.
SILVIA: OK. Tell me what's going on. I know things haven't been
  going well for Dad lately, but that's all.

From upstairs we hear Mother's voice.

MOTHER: Teresa! Teresa!
TERESA: Yes, ma'am. What is it?
MOTHER: Please come here.
SILVIA: Don't go.
TERESA: You know how she is when she gets mad.
SILVIA: Make her come here.
MOTHER: *(From above)* Teresa! Did you hear me?
TERESA: Yes, ma'am, I'm coming. Silvia just arrived. *(Pause.)*
MOTHER: Tell her I'll see her tomorrow. Show her to her room and then come.
TERESA: Yes, ma'am. Sergio's here, too, but he already went to bed.
MOTHER: Tell them not to go to bed yet. I'll be right down.
TERESA: Yes, ma'am.

Teresa pours more drinks.

TERESA: May you enjoy your days here. Cheers.
SILVIA: Cheers. *(Pause.)*

> *Silvia and Teresa maintain an air of*
> *expectation. Steps are heard from the second*
> *floor. Silvia and Teresa look toward the*
> *stairs, where a mature woman is descending.*
> *The Mother was beautiful in her youth; she*
> *is wearing a black dress with long sleeves and*
> *high collar, and black stockings; she carries a*
> *fan. She is attempting elegance. She comes*
> *down smiling, sure of herself. She holds out*
> *her hand to Silvia.*

MOTHER: Silvia, love, how are you. . .

> *The Mother kisses Silvia on the cheek, as if*
> *they were friends.*

SILVIA: Fine, Mom, thank you. *(The Mother sits down.)*
MOTHER: What heat, Tere. Turn on the fan.

Teresa obeys and the ceiling fan begins to turn. The Mother fans herself.

MOTHER: Where's Sergio? I thought he was with you.

TERESA: I'll call him. He might have gone to sleep.

MOTHER: *(To Silvia)* You look good.

SILVIA: You too, Mom.

MOTHER: What are you two drinking?

TERESA: Some Chinguere that Sergio brought me. Would you like some?

MOTHER: I don't drink alcohol. It's terrible for the skin. Bring me something cold, Tere.

TERESA: A coconut?

MOTHER: Fine. I'll just take a few sips. They're very fattening. And at sea level, the body absorbs liquids too easily. *(Teresa exits.)*

MOTHER: How have you been?

SILVIA: Fine, Mom, and you?

MOTHER: Wonderful. Except for this damned heat and these bloody mosquitoes. What a calamity. They should exterminate them for good. We don't need them on earth. They only cause problems and they're entirely in the way. Don't you agree?

SILVIA: Doesn't that dress make you hotter?

MOTHER: How's the little girl? I'd really like to see her.

SILVIA: Let me tell you how communication works: I ask a question and you answer, and then you ask and I answer. What do you say?

MOTHER: Why did you say that? I was just asking about your daughter.

SILVIA: She's fine.

MOTHER: You should have brought her. I'll bet she's beautiful. When are you going to bring her to Morelia?

SILVIA: Whenever you invite me.

MOTHER: Silvia, you're acting very strange.

SILVIA: You think so? You are too.

MOTHER: You're probably tired from the trip. Mexico's so far. How long was the trip?

SILVIA: Yes, I'm tired and I think I'll go to bed.

MOTHER: See how you are? When I want to get close to you, you reject me or run away.

SILVIA: Do you really want to talk or do you just need someone to listen to you?

MOTHER: Don't use that tone of voice with me. You act like I'm your enemy or. . .

SILVIA: Well, the truth is. . .

Teresa enters with the coconut.

TERESA: Here you are, ma'am. I hope you like it.

MOTHER: Thank you, Tere. *(She drinks.)* It's delicious. But I won't give in. I'll just take three little sips.

SILVIA: *(To Teresa.)* I'm going to bed. Would you come with me?

TERESA: I'll be right back, ma'am.

MOTHER: You're going to just leave me here? What manners. It's one thing for Silvia to do it, but you, Teresa? It's not right.

SILVIA: You stay. I'll go by myself.

MOTHER: Go with her, Teresa. Get her bed ready, put on clean sheets, put out her cold cream. Prepare her bath, dry her off, brush her hair, talk to her while she falls asleep. Go on. Take her mother's place, as always. *(The Mother gets up and goes toward the hallway.)*

MOTHER: Sergio, Sergio. . . Where are you, Sergio? *(She knocks at the first door. She pushes it. It moves and then falls, breaking a piece of the door frame. The Mother is startled and upset.)* I barely touched it.

TERESA: It was already broken. Matias has put off fixing it.

Sergio appears in the hallway dressed only in his underwear.

SERGIO: What's all this shouting, lady? Aren't you ashamed? What will the tourists say? *(They embrace and kiss.)*

MOTHER: My love, how are you? You've gotten more handsome.

SERGIO: And you've gotten younger.

MOTHER: Don't be silly. Don't I wish?

SERGIO: Let's see. Hug me again. *(They embrace again. They sit down in the vestibule.)*

MOTHER: I've been so worried about you. Have you been well?

SERGIO: Better than ever.

MOTHER: Why didn't you let me know you were coming? And how did you get out? Are you all right? I would have gone after you.

SERGIO: I thought Dad would have told you. He sent for me. And I did go to Morelia, but they told me you were here, with him.

MOTHER: Do you need anything?

SERGIO: Just you.

MOTHER: Don't joke about that. I might believe it.

SERGIO: Really. I need for us to be together. Would you stay here, to live with me?

MOTHER: The things you say! Would you like a little refreshment? The coconut is still cold.

Matias comes in from the swimming pool.

MATIAS: Here are the flowers, ma'am.

MOTHER: They're beautiful. *(She receives them and smells them. She makes a face and throws them aside. She feels nauseated.)* They're rotten.

MATIAS: But, ma'am. . .

MOTHER: They smell like death. And they're not from the magnolia tree.

MATIAS: But I just cut them.

MOTHER: Take them away, far away. They'll stink the place up.

SERGIO: Did you hear her? Take them away.

Matias picks up the flowers.

MATIAS: I don't know what happened. They were white. And fresh. And they smelled like perfume. Someone switched them on me. They're not the same ones. *(He goes out toward the pool.)*

MOTHER: *(To Sergio)* Let's talk. Would you like to walk along the beach?

SERGIO: Yes, let's walk.

TERESA: Mr. Garza wants to see everyone here tomorrow. He told me he would be waiting at nine.

MOTHER: So early? He's crazy.

> *Sergio and the Mother leave, holding hands,*
> *heading toward the sea. As they disappear,*
> *their laughter is heard.*

TERESA: They get along well. *(Pause.)* I'll be right back.

SILVIA: Where are you going?

TERESA: I'm going to take your father his bottle.

SILVIA: Don't give him any more. He'll be sick.

TERESA: If I don't take it to him, he'll come down for it.

SILVIA: I'd like to see him. I'll go with you.

TERESA: Go to bed. You'll see him tomorrow. He doesn't want to see you now.

> *Teresa climbs the stairs. Silvia goes to Teresa's room. The stage is empty for a moment. Then Matias enters, from the pool.*

MATIAS: What's going on? Where is everybody? The missus was here and Sergio over there. Teresa was sitting in that chair and Silvia. . . *(He looks down the hallway, toward the parking lot and then up the stairs. He shrugs his shoulders.)* Oh, well, they've all left. As always. . .

> *He exits. Darkness.*

II

> *Sergio, Silvia, Mother and Teresa are seated in the vestibule. Matias comes and goes, watering plants near the swimming pool. It is mid-morning.*

MATIAS: *(Looking toward the beach)* There he comes. Didn't I tell you? I saw him when he took off toward the cliff.

> *Silvia and Sergio get up and look toward the beach.*

SERGIO: That's not him.

MATIAS: Of course it is. That's Mr. Garza. Who else could it be?

SILVIA: That's not my Dad.

TERESA: *(Coming closer to them)* What's the matter? That's him. He's just a little thinner. And you're not used to seeing him without his suit and tie, that's all.

MATIAS: *(Shouting off)* Mr. Garza! Mr. Garza! We're over here.

SILVIA: *(Returning to her seat)* You're right, it must be the clothes that make him look like he's changed.

MOTHER: Finally. The master strolls along the beach, while we wait here like idiots. *(Long pause.)*

Garza arrives and waits by the entrance. He
is dressed informally, appropriately for the
climate. He has not shaved in several days.

GARZA: Sorry. I went walking down the beach and when I
remembered to look at my watch I saw it was very late. *(Silvia*
goes to him.) How are you, Silvia?

SILVIA: Fine, Dad. And you?

GARZA: I get by. *(He goes to Sergio and embraces him.)* It's good
to see you, son.

SERGIO: It sure is, Dad.

SILVIA: You're awfully thin. Aren't you eating right?

GARZA: Same as always.

SILVIA: Why don't you shave? You'd look younger. Or are you
sick?

MOTHER: Well, then. Why have you gathered us here?

GARZA: *(He sits down.)* I wanted to see everyone together, here
where we've been so happy together.

MOTHER: Happy? When?

SILVIA: I was. Every time we came here on vacation.

MOTHER: But I wasn't, and neither was your brother. Who likes to
come to this God-forsaken hotel for weeks on end? If it were a
nice hotel in Acapulco or Puerto Vallarta, that would be
different. But here?

GARZA: This isn't a God-forsaken hotel.

MOTHER: Of course not. It's a five-star luxury hotel, with a private
airport and a yacht club.

GARZA: It was a good hotel. The best one in these parts.

SERGIO: It's been destroyed.

MOTHER: Have you forgotten about the time you almost died from a
scorpion bite? Or about when you had a sunstroke and broke
out in welts? It has always been a horrible hotel. That's why
when you were small I never liked to bring you all here.

SILVIA: If you hated it so much, why did you come?

GARZA: Your father insisted. Once, poor Sergio was red as a lobster,
just from the indirect sunlight he got on the beach. His skin
fell off little by little.

SERGIO: I don't remember that.

MOTHER: But I do. *(To Garza)* Well, here we are.

GARZA: I want to tell you the truth about our situation. Because, I
imagine that you more or less know what it's all about.

SERGIO: I only know what's been published in the papers, but I don't
believe what they say.

SILVIA: Teresa told me a little and I hope it's nothing serious.

GARZA: It's serious. But there's a way out. I wanted to get you together to tell you the truth about all this. My truth.

MOTHER: And it had to be here, nowhere else?

GARZA: Yes, here, nowhere else. There was no better place. I can't stay in Morelia. They'd be after me all the time. And besides, we can rest here, spend a few days together. This was the first piece of property I got through my own effort. My business life started here. We'll be fine here.

SILVIA: I can't stay long. I have to return to Mexico, to my job.

SERGIO: Why'd you quit the Bank?

GARZA: I had political problems. The press, my enemies, the union, basically everybody was against me. Well, they weren't exactly against me. Since the General died, all of us who were in his group have had problems. They've tried to come between us, break us up, so that we wouldn't have any strength. I was the scapegoat. The president asked for my resignation, with the pretext that they were going to move the main office to Mexico.

MOTHER: What does that have to do with your personal matters? Why did they freeze your accounts in the other banks?

GARZA: That's standard procedure. When you resign amidst problems, there's an investigation. But they couldn't prove anything.

SERGIO: I hope your businesses haven't been jeopardized.

GARZA: I don't have any. When I took charge of the Bank, I sold them, to avoid criticism.

MOTHER: But you have the money.

GARZA: I invested it. . . poorly. Then came the devaluation, before it was supposed to. I made some errors in calculation.

MOTHER: You have a lot of companies that aren't in your name. They can't get at those.

GARZA: There are some problems with my partners. Since things are in their names now they want to keep everything. But I have my lawyers working on that. It's going to be a long haul, but I'll get all of that back.

SERGIO: Those bastards!

MOTHER: You still have money in the United States.

GARZA: What makes you think that?

MOTHER: I'm sure of it.

GARZA: Do you know what you're saying?

MOTHER: You sent a lot of dollars out, lots of them.

GARZA: You know that's not true.

MOTHER: You know it is true.

GARZA: If it were, we wouldn't be here. I would've gone to the U.S. a long time ago, like all the others.

MOTHER: I don't know why you haven't.

GARZA: Why are you lying? I may have a lot of faults, but I don't send my money abroad.

MOTHER: What about the check you gave me when I went to Houston? It was drawn on an American bank.

GARZA: I opened that account just for that trip. So you could get yourself and Sergio checked out.

SILVIA: Are you the only one with these problems? How about the General's other friends?

GARZA: For the moment, it looks like I'm the only one. It always happens at the beginning of a new term. They look for scapegoats and the chain breaks at the weakest link. That was me. But I'm sure that in a few months they'll sweep it all under the carpet and that will be the end of it. That's the way it works.

SILVIA: You'd better tell us everything, Dad.

GARZA: That's everything. I still have my political aspirations. I've always wanted to be governor of my state. Do you think I'd risk my career doing stupid things? I'll try to revindicate myself during the next term. The tide will turn. In my favor. You'll see.

SILVIA: And in the meantime, what can we do?

GARZA: I want your understanding.

SERGIO: You've got it.

GARZA: And I want your material help.

MOTHER: Money? If you don't have any, how do you expect us to?

GARZA: Not money, something else. It all depends on what Teresa accomplishes today. There's going to be a conference in the Port and they'll be inaugurating the new Convention Center. The Governor, the Secretary of Tourism and a lot of bigwigs from Mexico will be there. Teresa knows the governor very well. She's going to try to get me an appointment with him and I'll go to see him at his hotel. If that's not possible, she'll give him a letter in which I explain my situation. He's my friend. He'll help me.

SERGIO: What are you going to ask him for? If you want, I can go with Teresa.

GARZA: That won't be necessary. First, I want him to stop the highway they're constructing from destroying this hotel. They've decided it has to go through here, but a telephone call from him and they'd turn it around, make it go past La Loma, and then it would even be beneficial for us. I've heard they're examining my properties here in the state to prove that I've gotten rich while I was in office. Have you ever heard anything so stupid? The Governor can make sure the report that's sent to the Public Registry doesn't do me any harm. He can do that. He has a direct line. I think with that everything will be settled.

SILVIA: Why don't you go to the United States until it all passes over?

GARZA: And let them make mincemeat of me? Never. Not that. I prefer to stay and defend myself.

SILVIA: They've all left, Dad. And, see? Time has passed and they've returned without any problems.

GARZA: I won't run away. I'm not a criminal. I was taught when I was young to face my problems head on. That's why I'm staying. To fight for my name.

SERGIO: And don't you have any other friends who can help you?

GARZA: I'm alone now. Everyone's afraid because of the new program of moral renovation and other such stupidities. No one wants to get involved. That's why I'm turning to my family. You're the only ones I can really trust. I can count on you, can't I?

SERGIO: Of course, Dad.

SILVIA: You don't even have to ask.

MATIAS: Confidence killed the cat. Confidence and lack of confidence. I used to be very trusting, until once, when I was a cattleman, going down the country highway, a robber attacked me. That's what happened to me.

GARZA: *(He goes to Teresa and hands her a letter.)* Here's the letter, Teresa.

TERESA: Give it to me later. I might lose it.

GARZA: Take it now. And be very careful with it. Our future is in it.

Teresa takes it, looks at it and gets up.

TERESA: I'm going to put it away in my room, I wouldn't want it to. . . *(She exits.)*

GARZA: Come down to the beach, I want to show you something.

Garza leaves, followed by Silvia and Sergio.
Mother stays in her place, watching them
leave. Matias comes up to her.

MATIAS: Come with us, ma'am.   They're going to show us something.

Mother takes a magazine from a table, lies
back in her chair and remains still, with the
magazine in her hands. Her dark glasses
prevent us from seeing if she is reading or
sleeping.

MATIAS: Don't stay here alone. *(Pause.)* It's not good to be alone, with no one to talk to and no one to see. Come with us. Or would you rather I stayed with you? *(Pause. Matias turns on the ceiling fan, which begins to move)* That's OK. Do what you want, but don't be surprised if you start to hear voices. There are a lot of lost voices around here.

He exits toward the beach.

III

Dusk. Fog is invading the area. At first, we
can't see the people or the objects, but little
by little they appear with an unreal quality.
Matias turns on the light. Mother, leaning
on a pillar, looks out at the sea; Sergio is
napping in an armchair; Mr. Garza is resting
in a rocker which he rocks rhythmically;
Silvia, seated on the floor, is playing a game
of cards. Matias is trying to make a broom
from palm leaves.

SILVIA: Let's play cards. . . *(Pause.)* Nobody wants to play a game? *(Pause.)* Don't tell me you've sworn them off? *(She continues to shuffle.)* What's the matter with everybody, huh? Don't worry. Teresa will be back and she'll bring good news. She's very smart and she'll know how to give it to the Governor. You'll see.

MOTHER: Maybe she'll run into friends and just take off.

SILVIA: *(Coldly)* To where, Mom?

MOTHER: Oh, around. Same as always.

MATIAS: Mrs. Garza, please don't lean on that pillar.

MOTHER: Come take a look at this.

SERGIO: *(From his seat)* What is it?

MOTHER: Balls of fire. They're jumping around and chasing each other.

SERGIO: It's probably some kids playing with torches.

MOTHER: No. They're like big balls rolling around, then they fly up, as if someone were playing with them. And they jump from that hill over to the gully. Now they're on the hill. And there are a lot of them.

GARZA: You're imagining things.

SILVIA: It's probably lights from some ranch or maybe where they're burning off a field.

MOTHER: They're on the hill.

SILVIA: Are you wearing your contact lenses?

MATIAS: Careful with that pillar.

MOTHER: They're balls of fire. Look how shiny they are. They move around as if they were alive.

GARZA: You sound like a child.

MOTHER: How strange. Something's going on.

SERGIO: It's just an optical illusion.

MOTHER: They're there. They're real. If you don't believe me, come look.

MATIAS: Listen to me, I'm telling you for your own good.

SILVIA: Oh, Mom, forget those things.

MOTHER: Why do you say "Oh, Mom"? Are you doubting me? Do you think I'm seeing things? Do you think I can't tell what's real? Fine. Don't pay any attention to me. It won't be the first time I say something and no one listens. My words are silent. I speak but my voice doesn't come out, doesn't reach anyone. It won't be the first time or the last.

GARZA: Why don't you just shut up?

MOTHER: Don't I even have the right to say what I feel?

MATIAS: Ma'am, please lean somewhere else.

MOTHER: I don't feel like it.

MATIAS: Don't say I didn't warn you.

*Mother continues to lean on the pillar where
the General's portrait hangs. The others get
up and back away from the pillar. They look
at the Mother strangely.*

MOTHER: Why are you all looking at me like that? What's the matter with you?

*The pillar starts to crack and squeak. The
Mother feels it and moves away a little. It
starts to crumble and finally falls, filling the
room with dust. A piece of the roof falls.
The dust covers the Mother, who little by
little can be seen standing in the dust as it
clears. The others, as if nothing had
happened, return to their places and resume
their same positions. Matias picks up the
General's portrait.*

GARZA: Is it all right?

MATIAS: The glass broke and the frame came apart. The picture got dirty and a little torn in some places. *(Matias wipes it off with his shirt and tries to fix the frame.)*

*Mother brushes off the dust which has
covered her. She walks through the rubble
and goes toward the sea.*

MATIAS: There's no water in the pool. And the sea is dangerous this time of night.

Mother disappears.

SILVIA: Let's play. . . *(Pause.)* Nobody wants to play a short game? Don't tell me you've sworn off cards?

*Everyone remains in the same place. Matias
fixes the portrait. Garza pours a drink.*

SILVIA: Make me one, too, Dad, OK?

SERGIO: Me too, please.

GARZA: You're going to drink? Didn't you say. . .
SERGIO: Why not? There's a lot to celebrate.

> *Garza serves them.*

SERGIO: Cheers, Dad.
GARZA: Cheers, son. But let's toast to something. To the General.
SILVIA: To everyone. To Teresa, to the deal, to the Governor, to everything turning out right, to our going back to being like we were.
GARZA: Yes, like we were.
SERGIO: To Blue Beach. To the good times. To the happy family.
MATIAS: To all that, cheers.
SILVIA: *(To Matias)* Here. Drink from my glass.
MATIAS: And my vitamins?
SILVIA: It won't matter. Take it.

> *Matias takes the glass and drinks. He finishes the contents. Garza serves more. Matias returns the glass to Silvia.*

GARZA: *(To Matias)* Sweep up this rubble immediately and take it away. It stinks.
MATIAS: It doesn't smell of anything.
GARZA: I say it stinks.
SILVIA: It's not the rubble, Dad. That smell is coming from the swamp.
MATIAS: The swamp is about to dry up. The water level has gone down. There aren't any lilies or wet leaves anymore, or any rotting nests.
SERGIO: But it still stinks.
MATIAS: The swamp is drying up. The crocodiles died. The sand doesn't move anymore. The swamp doesn't smell anymore.
GARZA: It stinks. I say it stinks. If not, where is that smell coming from?
SERGIO: Maybe it's the gas. *(To Matias)* Go check the tanks.
MATIAS: We don't have any tanks anymore. Not even for the swimming pool. None.
GARZA: Well, then, it's you that stinks.
SILVIA: It's probably a skunk that passed by or a dead dog on the highway.
SERGIO: It's the sea. The beach was full of poisoned fish.
MATIAS: It's the dead people.

SERGIO: What dead people?

MATIAS: Go look at them. They're in the rooms on the other side, the ones that fell down during the earthquake.

GARZA: You dreamed that.

MATIAS: All gringos. Old man gringos and old woman gringas who came to spend their vacation here and got caught in the earthquake. We couldn't get them out. Teresa said we should leave them there, said they didn't need graves if they already had roofs and hotel walls around them.

GARZA: Why don't you go to bed?

SILVIA: Do you want more? *(She hands him her glass. Matias drinks.)* Get some rest.

MATIAS: I don't rest. I don't want to rest now. I'll get plenty of rest when I die. And that day is still a long way off. *(He takes the portrait of the General.)*

GARZA: Where are you taking that?

MATIAS: I'm going to see if I can fix it. Or do you want me to put it back up like this? *(He leaves.)*

SILVIA: How much did the General used to pay you?

GARZA: When? When I managed his ranch in Aldama or when I was his sidekick in Mexico or when we built this highway or during the campaign or when I was his chauffeur?

SILVIA: How much did he used to pay you to get women for him?

GARZA: Maids for his house, secretaries for his office or the female vote during the elections?

SILVIA: How much did he used to pay you to take broads to him on the Aldama ranch? Where did you find them? Did you bring them from other towns or were they from the village? Did you tell them who they were going to sleep with or was it a surprise? Did they go of their own free will?

GARZA: They went of their own free will.

SERGIO: The General wasn't exactly handsome.

GARZA: But he was a hero and any woman feels proud to sleep with a hero.

SILVIA: Not me.

GARZA: Because you've never had one near enough.

SERGIO: Heroes don't exist.

GARZA: The General existed.

SILVIA: Like you and like me. Flesh and blood.

GARZA: He was different. Without him there wouldn't be any history in this country. It's as if he were from another world. He would stare at you and know exactly what you were thinking. He always knew the right thing to say at the right moment. There were no problems that couldn't be solved. He would sit down to eat on the ground with the Indians in their huts. He knew how to put the gringos in their places every time they tried any funny stuff with us. Rich and poor, the right and the left, they all adored him. That's a hero. When he died, the whole country cried.

SILVIA: When you all went to the funeral, I remember that our nanny said, "So the old goat finally died." What old goat? I asked her. That damned Communist; now he's probably burning in hell for being evil, for being an atheist, for destroying the priests.

GARZA: Your nanny was an old woman who didn't know what she was talking about.

SILVIA: Is it true that that's when Mom lost her mind?

GARZA: Your mother is as sane as you are.

SILVIA: I was told that she was in mourning a long time and that she cried every day.

GARZA: We all cried.

SERGIO: You? Why? I thought he had turned his back on you a long time before that.

GARZA: Because others deceived him. I was framed and I was never able to clear my name. When I realized what was happening, it was too late to regain my status with him. It was my fault. I wasn't quick enough.

SILVIA: And you still defend him?

GARZA: I owe him everything.

SERGIO: Too bad you fell from his good graces.

GARZA: Yes, it was a shame. When I was in his good graces I always felt secure, even when there were problems.

SERGIO: If he were alive now, do you think he'd help you?

GARZA: Of course he would. He always helped me through the difficult times. He also intervened for you.

> *Some sharp, faraway sounds are heard. They are brought in with the wind and then they disappear.*

SILVIA: What's that?

GARZA: Nothing. A radio somewhere.

SERGIO: It sounds like women shouting.

> *The sounds increase. They sound like crying;*
> *the sound comes closer.*

SERGIO: Women crying.
GARZA: You hear some strange noises by the sea sometimes. It could be sea lions or walruses in heat.
SILVIA: *(Going toward the pool)* How strange. I'll go see. *(She exits.)*

> *The sounds increase and seem to be quite*
> *near. Now they sound like the squawking of*
> *birds fighting among themselves and circling*
> *the hotel. The noise is deafening. Sergio*
> *and Garza twist their bodies and faces trying*
> *to locate the noise.*

SERGIO: Women. Women crying. Listen, Dad.

> *The sound is carried farther away by the wind.*
> *Sergio stares at the panes of the pictures*
> *windows near the pool, which reflect lights*
> *and shadows. Through them he thinks he*
> *can make out the bodies of two women and*
> *several men.*

SERGIO: There they are. On the sand. Next to the pirul tree. Poor things. *(Pause. Sergio takes a piece of wood that Matias left behind and starts to beat on the panes.)* Stop it, you jerks! Leave them alone! Let them go! *(Garza goes to him and holds him. He hugs him. Pause.)* Poor women. . . poor . . .
GARZA: Come on. It's OK. Let's sit over here. You're tired. *(They sit. Garza embraces him tenderly. Sergio cries quietly. Long pause.)*
SERGIO: Why didn't you pay them?
GARZA: I don't know what you're talking about.
SERGIO: The ransom, Dad. Why didn't you give it to them?
GARZA: I paid it.
SERGIO: That's not true.
GARZA: I tell you I did pay it. You can believe me or not.
SERGIO: Then why didn't they let us go?
GARZA: How do I know? Those people are crazy. Beyond the law. Nothing matters to them.

SERGIO: Are you sure you paid them?

GARZA: Drop it. I paid it, and it was quite a sum.

SERGIO: How much, Dad?

GARZA: A fortune. I had to take everything out of the bank and borrow from my friends. Even the General loaned me money.

SERGIO: If you had paid them they would have let us go and they wouldn't have taken us so far away. It was so far away.

GARZA: I know.

SERGIO: Farther than the General's ranch. You know those gullies on the other side of the river?

GARZA: Sure. I used to go hunting over there.

SERGIO: Have you been in the sand pit near the stream?

GARZA: I think so.

SERGIO: They kept us there all night. Poor girls.

GARZA: I don't mean to blame them, but they were asking for it. Decent women don't get into the cars of young drunk men and go to the mountains with them. Especially at night.

SERGIO: We tricked them. They were beside the highway, near the interchange, waiting for the bus that goes to their neighborhoods, and we offered them a ride. At first they didn't want to go, they didn't trust us, but when they saw I was the one driving, they got in. Why wouldn't they get in with Mr. Garza's son and his friends? Did you ever go to the Lookout?

GARZA: Lots of times, but not to do what you guys were doing.

SERGIO: We were just about to take them home, when they knocked on our windows and made us get out.

GARZA: You shouldn't have opened the door, much less gotten out.

SERGIO: We thought they were policemen or workers of yours. They were after me, Dad. I was the one they were interested in.

GARZA: They wanted my money.

SERGIO: They wanted revenge. What had you done to them?

GARZA: How do I know? We don't even know who they were.

SERGIO: You should know, since they're your enemies.

GARZA: I wish I did know. Then I could have covered my ass in time and I wouldn't be in this mess.

SERGIO: They tied us up to the pinzan trees and the girls to the big pirul tree. You know which pirul I mean?

GARZA: Forget all that.

SERGIO: Why should I forget it?

GARZA: It's all over. If you're feeling bad and you've started to remember it all again, you can go back to the clinic for another treatment. Or we can fly a doctor down to see you here.

SERGIO: Poor girls. Don't you feel sorry for them?

GARZA: Of course I do. But, what can we do now?

SERGIO: They shouted, they cried, they screamed, but not like people. It seemed like they were killing them. Help us, for God's sake, they shouted. I closed my eyes, but I kept on seeing them with their torn clothes, their bloody faces, defending themselves by biting. Time moved slowly, very slowly, Dad. When they were through with them, they started beating us and taking our clothes off. Why didn't you give them the money?

GARZA: I told you I did. We left it at the Lookout, just like they asked.

SERGIO: Why didn't they let us go?

GARZA: They're crazy. Do you hear me? After they get their money they keep on committing atrocities. They're criminals. The police promised me they'd kill them on the spot if they caught them. I also paid the police.

SERGIO: Did they kill them?

GARZA: I don't know. Maybe not. They probably just took my money.

SERGIO: But you didn't pay the ransom, did you? *(Pause.)* Have you been in the sand pits near the stream? Have you seen those pinzan trees and the pirul tree?

> *Silvia arrives carrying a dead, bloody sea gull.*

SILVIA: Look. *(She throws it in the lobby.)*

> *The three of them look at the bird, first with revulsion and then with pity. Silvia takes it toward the maids' quarters. She returns with a towel in her hand, drying herself. She puts the towel on the floor, sits on it, takes the deck of cards. She plays. Sergio and Garza drink. Mother arrives from the beach. Her hair and clothing are wet, as if she had been in the sea.*

SILVIA: You'll catch cold. Dry your hair.

MOTHER: I'm fine like this. It's hot out.

SILVIA: Dry off with my towel. *(She goes to her and starts to dry her hair. Suddenly she is surprised.)* What's on your ear and your neck?

MOTHER: *(Pulling away brusquely.)* Nothing. Leave me alone. I'm sunburned.

SILVIA: That's not a sunburn.

MOTHER: Then it must be spots, from so many mosquitoes around here.

SILVIA: Your whole neck is covered in spots.

MOTHER: I'm telling you it's nothing. I'll go to my room and put a cream on it.

SILVIA: You don't have to hide anything from me.

MOTHER: I'm not trying to hide anything from you or from anybody.

SILVIA: Is that why you wear those dresses?

MOTHER: I wear those dresses because I like them. I look thinner and younger in them.

SILVIA: Please, Mom. I'm not an idiot who can't understand things.

SERGIO: Leave her alone.

MOTHER: You've always been prone to exaggeration. I'll see everyone tomorrow. Sleep well.

SILVIA: Mom, you're completely covered with the stuff. Is that why you use that makeup and those stockings?

MOTHER: Don't you know anything about fashion? Don't you look at the magazines?

SILVIA: What do you gain by pretending?

MOTHER: Pretending what?

SILVIA: You know.

MOTHER: I have a simple vitamin deficiency. Do you understand? When I don't take my vitamins on time, this happens to me.

SILVIA: That's not true.

SERGIO: What difference does it make to you?

MOTHER: I would be the first to worry if it were anything else. I'd find a doctor in Mexico City or I'd go to the United States. How horrible, if I had what you're thinking. When I first came to Tierra Caliente with your father, he took me to see some harpists and dancers. The musicians played "balonas" and the women danced alone on platforms, holding their enormous skirts. Several men on horseback were riding around them, and they made their horses dance for them. I thought it was a funny custom. Until your father explained to me that they had *quiricua* and that's why they had to dance far away and on their horses. It's a disease from Tierra Caliente. Fortunately, I'm

from a very cold region. *(Pause.)* *Quiricua.* How horrible.
I'm going to my room to change. You're right, I'll catch cold.
SERGIO: I'll go with you, Mom.
MOTHER: Why, son? You stay here. I'll be back.
SERGIO: I'm going with you. *(Mother and Sergio go up the stairs.)*

> *Silvia pours herself and her father drinks.*
> *Garza is seated. Silvia sits at his feet and*
> *leans her head against his legs.*

SILVIA: Where did you meet her?
GARZA: In Guadalajara.
SILVIA: Where, exactly?
GARZA: I think it was at a dance. Then I invited her another day to
the movies and she accepted, with the condition that we first go
to mass. I accepted and then we kept on seeing each other.
Back in those days it was the custom to stand in the street
outside a woman's house and she would talk to you from
inside. Then I met the General and he invited me to work on
the highway that they were going to build from the coast to
there. I had to come here, so we got married. It was a hurried
wedding.
SILVIA: None of that is true. I know where you met her and why
you came here.
GARZA: It's exactly as I said. If you know a different story, you
know more than I do.
SILVIA: One night, at a party in Mexico City, someone asked me if I
knew you, when I said I was from Tierra Caliente. I told them
I didn't and they started to talk about you. They told me about
how you met Mom and why you came to work in Tierra
Caliente.
GARZA: And you believed them?
SILVIA: At first I was angry. I thought they were lying. Then I
suddenly understood a lot of things, and then I thought it was
funny, very funny. The truth is I can't imagine Mom. How
did you manage to transform her? You overdid it. Now she's
so refined, so educated, putting on the airs of a princess.
GARZA: You shouldn't judge her.
SILVIA: I'm not judging her. I simply can't understand how she
could change so much. Whoever sees her now. . .
GARZA: Whatever they told you, it's not true. I have a lot of
enemies. They invent things to make people think ill of me.
SILVIA: I'm a big girl now, Dad. Why hide things from me?

GARZA: I'm not hiding anything. I've led a clean life. I don't have anything to be ashamed of. *(Pause. Silvia stares at the ceiling, toward a corner.)*
SILVIA: Look.

Garza looks at the indicated spot. A few pieces of rubble fall from the ceiling, leaving streams of dust.

GARZA: Those beams are rotten. I'll tell Matias to fix it.
SILVIA: Yeah. Tell Matias. *(Pause.)* I would like to be in a bordello, but not as a visitor.
GARZA: Don't say such stupid things.
SILVIA: I'd like to work in one, for one night or one week. Maybe a month. It must be interesting. How many people visit it per night? I'd like to see what the Guadalajara bordello is like. Does it still exist?
GARZA: You're soft in the head.
SILVIA: Did it have a red light? Where were the rooms? Who controlled them? Was it a dirty place? Was there music? How much did they charge? Did you go several times? How much did you have to pay to get her out? You did have to pay, didn't you?
GARZA: Why are you playing this game?
SILVIA: Playing?
GARZA: Yes, making up those stories.
SILVIA: They're not stories.
GARZA: They're falsehoods, slander, or whatever you want to call it. What do you gain by inventing such things?
SILVIA: So now it's all a product of my imagination, of my evil desires.
GARZA: That's right. You've never loved your mother. She's a good woman.
SILVIA: A good woman. I've been watching you two since I was a girl. I know what you are like and what she's like. I'm not a guest.
GARZA: You have a filthy mind.
SILVIA: They told me my mother was in love with the General. That you loaned her to him in exchange for favors. That she fell in love with the General and that's when you started hating her.
GARZA: That's a dirty lie. It was an impeccable friendship. He respected your mother very much.

SILVIA: And you?

GARZA: He respected everyone.

MATIAS: *(Entering)* It's true. I've always respected everyone, but no one respects me. Well, some do, like Silvia, but no one else does. They don't want to see me, they hide from me. They're in one place, I hear them talking, I go over there, but I get there and they're gone. Sergio was just in his room. I knew it, clear as day. I went to take him some soap and when I went in, he had disappeared. Mrs. Garza was by the swimming pool yesterday looking at the camellias and scolding me because according to her I've let them dry up. It's not true, ma'am, it's not true, I told her. Let me explain. And she left, without even hearing me out. And Teresa, well, it goes without saying. I hear her singing, drunk, like always, and when I look for her to tell her to shut up, to let me sleep, I can't find her. I go all over the hotel following her singing, I open the rooms, I go upstairs, I go out on the terrace, I look for her in the basement and I can't even find her shadow; but she keeps on singing. Why does she hide from me? Everyone hides from me. Why don't they want to look at me? Why does everyone do this to me?

SILVIA: Go out to the highway. See if Teresa's coming.

MATIAS: Will you all stay here?

GARZA: Yes, we'll be here.

MATIAS: Really? You'll be here all night? And tomorrow, when I wake up, will you be sitting here just like now?

GARZA: Don't worry. We'll always be here. Either here or on the beach.

MATIAS: And Teresa too?

SILVIA: She shouldn't be long now. Go find her. That'll please her.

> *Matias exits toward the parking lot. Long pause. The noise of dogs barking can be heard. Mother and Sergio come down the stairs. Mother has changed her dress.*

MOTHER: Here comes Teresa.

> *Everyone looks toward the parking lot. Teresa enters. Garza goes to her.*

GARZA: What happened?

MOTHER: You're drunk.

TERESA: Just happy.

GARZA: Did you get to speak to him?

TERESA: There were so many people you couldn't even get in.

SILVIA: What did he say?

TERESA: All of Michoacan was there, plus all the people who came down from Mexico, plus the party crashers from around here, plus. . .

SERGIO: Did you give him the envelope?

TERESA: All the congressmen and Miss Michoacan. Even the Bishop was in the soup. I ran into the Galvez family and they wouldn't even say "hi" to me. As if I had cooties. . .

GARZA: What about my problem? The rest doesn't interest me.

SILVIA: Let her tell her story, Dad.

MOTHER: We're not interested in what happened to her.

TERESA: The truth is, it was very difficult to get near the Governor. Everyone wanted to talk to him.

GARZA: Did you talk to him or not?

TERESA: Please, don't shout at me. I'm not deaf.

SILVIA: Calm down, Teresa.

GARZA: The only thing I want is for you to focus on what happened with the envelope.

TERESA: Well, OK, sir. I did manage to speak to him. He recognized me immediately. He said, "What's up, Teresa? How's everything at La Loma?" Fine, I said; and there I stood, alone, whistling, as the song says. He laughed, took me by the arm and said, "I haven't forgotten that seafood dinner you prepared for us. I've never seen such big oysters." You still remember that? I asked him. That was a thousand years ago. "Not so long," he said. "Just a term as congressman, a term as senator and one as governor." And he started laughing. So I thought, this is the right moment, and I let him have it. Mr. Garza wants to see you. "How is he?" he asked me. You can imagine, I told him. "What a shame," he said, "What a shame I can't do anything to help him. This is a federal matter, the orders come from Mexico and I have to obey, you know." I gave him the letter and he said "I'll read it with pleasure, but tell him I don't promise anything. Just my friendship, which he'll always have in spite of everything." And then the crowd closed in on us and took him away from me.

GARZA: Didn't you follow him? Didn't you try to talk to him some more?

TERESA: It was impossible.

SILVIA: Nothing's ever been impossible for you, Teresa.

TERESA: This time it was. I couldn't do anything.

SERGIO: So then, you spent your time getting drunk.

TERESA: What'd you think? That I was going just as a messenger pigeon, just to take that letter? Everyone was drinking. I wasn't going to stand around just watching. I had to pretend, stay there somehow, try and see if there was anything else I could do. Suddenly, he disappeared with his people, along with Miss Michoacan. They must have taken the party somewhere else.

MOTHER: In conclusion, there's nothing to be done.

GARZA: Sure there is. Didn't you hear? He confirmed his friendship. He promised to read the letter. Things are going well, don't you think, Silvia?

SILVIA: Who knows? It depends.

GARZA: Don't be like that, so defeatist. I seem like the young one and you all the old ones. We have to keep moving forward. Everything's going well. Don't you see? This is the beginning. Good job, Teresa. Good job. It didn't turn out exactly as we'd hoped, but it's not the end either. There's hope, don't you see? There's a lot of hope.

TERESA: Let me finish telling you. They told me that the highway is going to go right through this hotel. That the Expropriation Decree is just about to be issued. That there's an order for your arrest and that any moment now they're going to put the screws to you, as soon as the warrant gets here. Many people asked me where you were hiding. I told some of them you were in Mexico City, others the United States, others to go fuck themselves. Did I do right?

GARZA: You're joking, right?

MOTHER: What a lack of respect. To joke about a thing like this. *(To Garza:)* But it's your fault. You've allowed her to treat you like this. You gave her wings.

SILVIA: Is all that true, Teresa?

TERESA: *(Makes a cross with her fingers and kisses it).* I swear by the cross. Let lightening strike me if I 'm lying. Why would I make it up?

SERGIO: Just to get back at us. That's all. To rub salt on our wounds.

TERESA: Hey! You know me better than that!

SILVIA: Shut up.

GARZA: All is not lost.

MOTHER: Didn't you hear? They're going to knock the hotel down. And they might arrest you.

GARZA: I can get an order of protection against the Decree and against the order of arrest. I'll look for a good lawyer who'll get me the protections. Nothing's happened here. Our plans can go on as before. I'll start over here. You all will help me.

SILVIA: What do you want us to do?

GARZA: Matias will clean the rooms. *(To Mother)* You'll take charge of the restaurant and the kitchen. Teresa will be in charge of maintenance and waiting tables, and the swimming pool; Silvia will keep the books, do the ordering, and take care of public relations. And Sergio will be the manager of it all. I'll teach him. This will be a family business like the kind there used to be and still are in Europe. We'll give the guests a lot of personal attention, the kind that have disappeared from hotels these days. The first few years will be difficult, but later on we'll try to hire more personnel, Indians from the area or women from the ranches, who can help us with the heaviest tasks. And then, if all goes well, we can even open a chain of similar hotels all along the coast.

> *Dense silence. Mother applauds wildly.*
> *Then her clapping becomes paused and slow,*
> *finally pathetic little claps. Silence again.*
> *Pause.*

MOTHER: Are you finished?

SILVIA: Don't make fun of him.

MOTHER: I don't know whether to laugh or cry over what you've said.

SILVIA: Don't you understand what this means?

MOTHER: Of course I do. But I don't plan to stay here and work, and neither does Sergio.

SERGIO: Yes, I do, Mom.

MOTHER: Don't tell me he's convinced you.

SERGIO: Yes, Mom. I'm gonna go for it.

MOTHER: Have you lost your mind? You can't live here. You'll die from this climate and all these animals. Surely you're not planning on becoming a boatman or a waiter.

SERGIO: Why not, Mom?

MOTHER: I think it's fine if you want to work and earn your own money. But not here. Come with me to Morelia. We'll start a business there. We can open a music store, with stereos and electronic things, for example. You like cars. How about an automobile accessory shop?

SERGIO: I prefer to stay here.

MOTHER: You need to see doctors. You're still not well.

GARZA: He's fine. I've been watching him.

MOTHER: I don't believe anything you say. I'll get my information from the clinic.

SERGIO: Really, Mom. I'm fine.

MOTHER: I don't believe you. I don't believe a word either you or your father say.

GARZA: What about you, Silvia? What do you think?

SILVIA: I'm happy you're so optimistic. I'm happy you don't feel defeated. I came here to invite you to come to Mexico to spend some time with me. I'm doing very well at my job. The offer's still good for whenever you want to come, but I couldn't live here, not now. Angela's still small.

GARZA: Are you still seeing that man?

SILVIA: No, but I'm getting organized all by myself and I plan to keep moving forward.

GARZA: You don't want to help me.

SILVIA: Try to understand, Dad. I can't. I just made the down payment on a condominium and I have to pay the monthly payments. Angela just started kindergarten and the company just made me manager of a branch office. Really, Dad. I can't.

GARZA: What about you, Teresa?

TERESA: This is your hotel and you can do what you want with it. But that wasn't the agreement. You told me I was going to be the manager.

GARZA: We'll all do it together.

TERESA: You didn't tell me I was going to be demoted from manager to maid. Don't change the rules of the game, Mr. Garza. You also told me Silvia had already agreed to come and now I see that's not true.

GARZA: I told you I was sure she'd agree, but if she can't do it, or doesn't want to, well, that doesn't change our plans.

SERGIO: You've been dipping into the kitty, that's what you don't want to give up, right, Teresa?

TERESA: I've taken care of all of this alone, without charging a cent.

SERGIO: But you were planning to charge, weren't you? You should be made to pay, for letting it go to ruin. This hotel is run down because of your poor administration. Right, Dad?

GARZA: Well, Teresa made a few mistakes, but all that's in the past now.

TERESA: How can you say that? For years I sent you all the profits punctually. All of you lived off this hotel and ate it all up. Have you forgotten that? The papers are inside.

GARZA: If you want, we can talk later, and settle accounts.

TERESA: Let's settle them now. Am I going to keep managing this or not?

GARZA: Why don't we do this? You and Sergio can manage it together.

SERGIO: No, Dad. One person will have to do it alone.

TERESA: If you won't even recognize all the work I've done, I'm out.

SILVIA: I recognize your work, but now there has to be a new organization. There have to be changes.

TERESA: Changes to screw me over. That's called ingratitude and I would be a fool to accept. That's what I've been. An old fool, just that. What have I ever been for you all? A member of the family? No. An employee? Not that either, since you've never paid me. A dependent? I've earned my food. A tourist. Absolutely not--no one's ever waited on me. What am I? A fool. That's all.

SILVIA: Tere, please be quiet. You're drunk.

MOTHER: You all haven't even begun to work and you're already at each other like cats and dogs. But, whatever. I'm planning to leave tomorrow morning, early. Could you come with me for just a moment, son?

SERGIO: I'll be right up, Mom.

MOTHER: I just need a word with you.

SERGIO: I'll be right there. *(To Silvia.)* You have to help, Silvia.

SILVIA: I can't.

SERGIO: We're talking about our family.

SILVIA: I have another family.

GARZA: Think it over, Silvia. Don't you believe in my projects?

SILVIA: Of course I do, but you should understand.

GARZA: I've never denied you anything. I always gave in to your whims. You've been able to do exactly what you wanted with your life. I let you go to Mexico, to the United States, to give up your studies, to live with whoever you wanted. Now I need your help. Think it over, please.

SILVIA: There's nothing to think about, Dad.

SERGIO: Let her go, Dad. Let's go to my room so you can see what I brought you. Remember that menthol shaving cream? You'll see. *(They exit.)*

SILVIA: What are you going to do?

TERESA: I'm going to Mexico with you.

SILVIA: My apartment's small. Angela and I barely fit. You can stay with us, of course, while you find a boarding house or an apartment to rent.

TERESA: You don't want me to live with you? I can help you with your little girl. What could be better than to have her godmother watch her?

SILVIA: You need to live alone, Teresa, so you can make your own life and have your own friends, like you've had here.

TERESA: I don't know anyone there. I'll feel better if I'm around people I know. I've lived here, exiled, for more than fifteen years. I'll feel alone in such a big city.

SILVIA: As sociable as you are, you'll have friends to spare.

TERESA: I don't want any other friends. I want to be near you, to live with you.

SILVIA: Please Teresa.

TERESA: Don't I even have the right to ask you?

SILVIA: Be quiet.

TERESA: Why should I be quiet? *(Long pause.)*

SILVIA: You're acting stupid.

TERESA: I am stupid. If I were smart I never would have served in this house like a dog all these years, never asking anything in return. What do I have to show for it?

SILVIA: Don't look at it like that. We've all had our troubles. What's more, let me think it over, OK? I'll write you. Or maybe later, when I have a house or a bigger apartment. . .

TERESA: Forget what I said. *(She walks toward the beach.)*

SILVIA: Where are you going? *(She watches her disappear. Then she sits in the rocker and rocks gently.)*

IV

Dawn. Garza, Sergio and Silvia are playing cards at the table in the lobby. They play in silence. The noise from the sea gets louder. Waves breaking on the rocks of the nearby beach can be heard. Matias comes running up from the beach.

MATIAS: Come quickly, come stop Teresa.
SILVIA: Where is she?
MATIAS: She's leaving. She went singing as far as the dock. It looks like she's drunk.

Silvia gets up and looks toward the sea.

GARZA: Let her do what she wants.
MATIAS: When she jumped into the boat I shouted to her that it didn't have any oars or a motor, but she didn't hear me.
SERGIO: She'll be back.
MATIAS: The sea is rough today. There's a lot of wind and the waves are big.
SERGIO: She knows how to swim. She'll swim back.
MATIAS: Do something. Teresa's being carried away by the waves.
GARZA: What do you want us to do?
MATIAS: Go get her. Catch up with her. You can still see her.
SERGIO: She left of her own free will.
MATIAS: I don't want her to go away. Who'll be in charge of the keys? Who's going to help me hold the walls up? Who's going to kill the bed bugs and the cockroaches?
SERGIO: You will.
MATIAS: And who'll give me my medicine? Who'll thread the needles?
GARZA: Shut up and get out of here. Go find some wood and nails and start fixing this.
MATIAS: What about Teresa? Isn't anyone going after her?
GARZA: If you love her so much, you go get her.
MATIAS: *(Going toward the beach)* Teresa... Teresa...

His voice disappears. The sound of the sea gets louder. The sound of the waves gets louder.

V

Afternoon. Silvia is looking toward the highway. Sergio and Garza continue playing and drinking.

SILVIA: They're cutting down the trees in the swamp and some men are taking measurements at La Loma.

GARZA: Good. The new highway will bring us some tourists.

SERGIO: It's going to go right through this table. I'll stay on the side where the sea is, and you can stay on the swamp side.

GARZA: They'll go around the hotel.

SERGIO: *(To Silvia.)* Find me a syringe.

SILVIA: There aren't any here.

SERGIO: How does the old man inject those vitamins you brought him?

SILVIA: They're capsules.

SERGIO: Capsules are tablets. Tablets can be crushed into powder. You put the powder in a tube. The tube has an opening, as small as the eye of a . . . *(He laughs.)*

GARZA: I'm going hunting in the swamp. I need the pistol.

SERGIO: You can frisk me. I don't have it.

GARZA: You took it away from Matias.

SERGIO: I gave it back to Teresa, didn't I, Silvia?

SILVIA: Yes.

GARZA: I think I have a syringe in my room.

SILVIA: Dad, please.

GARZA: Are you going to stay with us?

SILVIA: No.

GARZA: Then mind your own business. *(To Sergio.)* I'll trade you the pistol for a syringe.

Mother enters.

MOTHER: Sergio is just a boy.

GARZA: He's grown a lot, a lot. He knows what he does.

MOTHER: Let's go, Sergio.

SERGIO: Can't you see how much nicer it is here? The sea, the gulls, the breeze. . . You can sleep peacefully here day and night.

MOTHER: If you don't come with me, you'll never see me again.

SERGIO: Really? Really? I'll come looking for you. And I'll bring you a fan.

MOTHER: You won't find me. *(She leaves.)*

SERGIO: *(He tries to follow her. He walks with difficulty.)* Yes I will. *(He sits again.)*

GARZA: Let's keep playing. Sit down, Silvia.

SILVIA: I'm tired of playing. *(She leaves.)*

Sergio and Garza are seated facing each other.
Garza pours liquor into the glasses.

GARZA: Cheers, son.

SERGIO: Cheers, Dad. To your prompt return to politics. They need you there. *(They drink. Sergio shuffles the cards.)*

GARZA: Shall we make the trade?

SERGIO: *(Laughing strangely)* Let's let the cards decide. *(They play.)*

VI

> *Midnight. Two big suitcases are on the floor. Matias appears with the General's portrait and hangs it on a pillar. The portrait is damaged and poorly hung. He comes and goes with different pieces of wood and a tool box. From the latter he takes a hammer and several nails. He starts to repair the wooden stairway that leads to the restaurant. We hear the sound of the hammer hitting the wood. The Mother comes down the stairs.*

MOTHER: Call Sergio.

MATIAS: He doesn't want to leave his room. You go. And tell him to give me my syringe back. Teresa bought it for me.

MOTHER: When he comes out give him this letter.

MATIAS: I'm not giving him anything. He doesn't pay any attention to me.

> *The Mother goes to the front desk.*

MOTHER: I'll leave it right here for him.

MATIAS: He's acting funny. Laughing all the time. He can't stop laughing. . .

MOTHER: And Silvia?

MATIAS: She's outside, warming the motor.

MOTHER: Why haven't you taken the luggage to the car?

MATIAS: They're heavy. What's in them?

MOTHER: None of your business.

MATIAS: Gold coins, rocks, bones?

MOTHER: You're a good-for-nothing. *(She takes the two suitcases and leaves.)*

MATIAS: And Mr. Garza, isn't he going with you?

> *Matias climbs the stairs looking for Garza.*
> *Long pause. Silvia comes in from the*
> *parking lot and sees Matias coming down the*
> *stairway.*

SILVIA: Tell Dad we're leaving.
MATIAS: He's asleep.
SILVIA: Wake him up.
MATIAS: I already called him. He won't move.

> *Silvia goes up the stairs. Matias follows*
> *her, with difficulty. Silvia comes down with*
> *a serious expression on her face.*

MATIAS: Are you leaving now? *(He follows her.)* When will you
be back? *(Silvia leaves hurriedly. Matias watches her leave
from the stoop.)* Good luck!

> *Matias returns to his work and continues*
> *repairing the stairway to the restaurant. He*
> *talks to himself, but we can't hear what he*
> *says. We hear the monotonous, rhythmic*
> *sound of the hammer hitting wood. From*
> *outside we hear the sound of sea birds and*
> *tropical animals. The sea can be heard in the*
> *distance. The waves break softly on the*
> *beach.*

THE END

One of the most surprising phenomena of the Mexican theater of the second half of the twentieth century has been the sudden arrival and success of **Tomás Urtusástegui.** Born in Mexico City in 1933, before 1980 he had never written a play; to date his dramatic production consists of more than sixty plays, including monologues, one-acts, two-acts, three-acts, and one very long and complex historical play which has seventy different characters. For those of us who know his plays, which tend to be satirical, farcical and scatological, perhaps even more surprising is his affirmation that in real life he is not funny: "I'm the straightest, driest person you will ever meet," he has said.

Urtusástegui's most successful plays have been *Do You Smell Gas?* (*¿Huele a gas?*), *Limited Capacity* (*Cupo limitado*) and *The Doubt* (*La duda*); the latter opened at a large theater in Mexico City in the summer of 1993 and ran until late May, 1994. Two other of Urtusástegui's plays have been translated into English, *Limited Capacity* and *Water*; the playwright has seen his plays performed in both Spanish and English in the United States, and travels frequently to other Latin American countries to see his works staged and to conduct theater workshops. *Do You Smell Gas?*, similarly to most of Urtusástegui's comedies, targets the hypocrisy of the Mexican upper middle class, exposing the stereotypes and prejudices that underlie so much of its discourse and behavior. Though culturally specific in many ways, this play's appeal is in most ways universal, its bawdy style reminiscent of such classics as Aristophanes and Rabelais; it requires very little introduction.

DO YOU SMELL GAS?

by Tomás Urtusástegui

CHARACTERS:

Mary (owner of the house), 40
Tony (her husband), 43
Laura (guest), 35
Jose Manuel (her husband), 38
Andrea (guest), 26
Paulino (her husband), 37
Jesus (waiter), 28

SET:

The action occurs during the present time. All of the characters except the waiter are upper middle class; nouveau riche, bourgeois and industrialists. They are all wearing formal attire. The women are laden with heavy jewels. No one looks elegant. The waiter is wearing a white shirt and dark pants.

Terrace of a residence. Picture windows look on to the garden. Wicker furniture. Table with foot warmer underneath, flower vase on top. A door, left, which leads to the rest of the house. Besides the large pieces of furniture, there are flower pots with plants, a portable bar and a tea cart. In the garden we can see a stone fountain.

Nighttime. The garden is illuminated. The terrace is dark. The waiter enters, turns on the lights. A moment later the lady of the house enters. She could be a foreigner; at least she tries to seem so by dying her hair blonde and using a lot of makeup. She is a little overweight. We can see that she is using a girdle.

*   *   *

MARY: *(Walking around the terrace, examining everything)* Is everything ready?

JESUS: Yes, ma'am.

MARY: And the ashtrays?

JESUS: I'll bring them right away.

MARY: Why do I have to remind you of everything?

JESUS: I'm sorry, ma'am.

MARY: When I give you the signal, bring out the coffee and the liqueur glasses.

JESUS: Yes, ma'am.

MARY: And watch out you don't break anything else.

JESUS: Nothing to worry about, ma'am.

MARY: *(Still examining everything)* Make sure the coffee is good and hot.

JESUS: Yes, ma'am.

MARY: *(Running her finger over the coffee table)* Dust! I told you to clean out here.

JESUS: I cleaned it this afternoon.

MARY: Obviously not very well. Hand me a rag!

JESUS: Whatever you say, ma'am.

MARY: *(Pointing to the bar)* The alcohol is in that cabinet.

JESUS: I understand, ma'am.

MARY: Bring the glasses out on the silver tray.

JESUS: Yes, ma'am.

MARY: I'm going in to my guests, now. Don't forget the ashtrays, the coffee, the glasses. During dinner you waited forever to clear away the dirty dishes. I don't want that again.

JESUS: Nothing to worry about, ma'am. Everything will be right where you want it.

MARY:*(Leaving)* I hope so. *(She shakes her head doubtfully.)*

*Jesus, very serious, watches her leave. When
she has gone he changes attitude. He dusts
the furniture indifferently, brings out an
ashtray and throws it anywhere carelessly.
He yawns. He goes to the bar and takes out a
bottle.*

JESUS: *(Holding up a bottle)* Yes, ma'am. Whatever you say, ma'am. *(Drinking straight from the bottle)* Cheers, ma'am.

*He puts the bottle down. He puts it in its
place, humming a popular tune. He lights a
cigarette. He opens the window which leads
to the garden. He leans against it. He
smokes his cigarette calmly. When he hears
voices he throws the cigarette out the
window, closes it and goes to stand, very
serious, in front of the entryway. The guests
enter in couples. They converse among
themselves.*

MARY: *(To Jose Manuel)* It was from a case of wine someone gave my husband for Christmas.

JOSE MANUEL: Delicious.

MARY: With this God-awful crisis, I doubt anyone will be giving away that kind of wine anymore. Oh well, we'll have to start drinking domestic wines.

ANDREA: *(To her husband, who is a Spaniard, somewhat bald. The difference in ages is apparent. He has been picking his teeth with a toothpick. In a hushed tone)* Put that toothpick away!

PAULINO: Says who?

ANDREA: I say. It's not proper.

PAULINO: *(Putting the toothpick in the pocket of his coat):* Bah!

MARY: *(Seating the guests)* Make yourselves comfortable, please. Are you OK, Laura dearest?

LAURA: Yes, I'm fine, thank you.

MARY: *(To Pauline and Andrea)* You two sit here.

ANDREA: Thank you.

LAURA: After all I ate tonight I'm not going to fit in this chair.

ALL THE GUESTS, IN UNISON: Dinner was delicious.

MARY: Thank you.

JOSE MANUEL: You're a wonderful cook, ma'am.

MARY: *(Smiling)* Please don't call me "ma'am." You make me feel old.

JOSE MANUEL: What do you mean "old"? You're the youngest one here. Right?

ALL THE GUESTS: Right.

MARY: You don't know how delighted I was when my husband told me you all were coming on my birthday; he couldn't have given me a nicer gift. *(They all smile widely, exaggerating.)* My, but he's taking a long time. *(To Andrea)* Whenever he starts talking to your father he loses track of time. It's a shame they couldn't stay.

ANDREA: They had a prior engagement.

MARY: Well, at least they came to dinner and left you with us. Having you is almost like having them here.

> *Andrea and Laura get up. They go to the windows that look on to the yard. They make the same movements, as if choreographed. They speak in unison.*

LAURA AND ANDREA: What a beautiful terrace!

MARY: Do you like it?

LAURA AND ANDREA: *(Leaning out of the window)* And what a view! I love it!

MARY: It's one of my husband's vices; he takes care of it himself.

> *While Mary is saying this last phrase, her husband enters. He smiles at what he hears.*

TONY: It's true, every day before going to the office I water all the plants myself.

LAURA AND ANDREA: Very beautiful! Positively beautiful! *(To their husbands)* Come see.

> *Paulino and Jose Manuel get up and in unison go to the picture window.*

PAULINO AND JOSE MANUEL: Very pretty.

MARY: The noise of the sprinkler calms my nerves; I can spend hours listening to the water fall. It's like a symphony.

ANDREA: The same thing happens to me with the noise of the ocean. It's a miracle to me that we survive in this city with so much noise and smog.

EVERYONE: It's horrible! The traffic is terrible! We're not safe! There's a shortage of water! The parks are being destroyed! There's garbage everywhere!

> *They enact a sort of ballet in which the music will be the above sentences, said in different tones and rhythms. All of their gestures will express disgust, horror or disdain. Upon finishing the ballet they sit down again at their places.*

PAULINO: This yard reminds me of that politician's garden, the one they just put in the slammer for fraud. Boy, did he deserve it!

JOSE MANUEL: How can you say that?

EVERYONE: Yes, how can you?

PAULINO: Well, I. . .

JOSE MANUEL: He's a friend of ours. A very honorable person, loyal to the government and to his friends. He was set up by the police.

PAULINO: They say he stole. . .

JOSE MANUEL: Stole, my eye! He took what was rightfully his. Wouldn't that be just dandy: you knock yourself out for everybody for years and years and then you don't even get a cut.

TONY: That's true. A politician only has six effective years in his lifetime. After that, how's he supposed to get by? Are you gonna support him?

PAULINO: Well, I. . .

MARY: Who says he stole?

PAULINO: Um, um. Everybody: the people.

MARY: They're just jealous.

PAULINO: What about the poor people?

MARY: They're poor because they want to be. Bums. Useless jerks. There's plenty of work out there, but nobody wants to work.

ANDREA: I haven't been able to get a laundry woman no matter what I offer to pay. Let's not fool ourselves: they don't want to work!

TONY: They expect the government to give them everything. That's the shape we're in! *(Changing the topic. To Mary:)* Dearest Mary, aren't you going to offer us coffee and cordials? *(Smiling.)* Our guests are going to say, and rightly so, that we're not good hosts.

GUESTS, TOGETHER: No, God no!

MARY: Excuse me. You seemed so involved in the discussion. But, of course, I'll see to it right now. *(Calling:)* Jesus! Jesus!

JESUS: *(Enters and approaches the group)* You rang, ma'am?

MARY: Please bring out the silver tray with the cordial glasses and then the cart with the coffee pot and cups.

JESUS: Right away, ma'am. *(He starts to leave. He returns.)* Shall I bring the sugar too, ma'am?

MARY: *(Forcing a smile)* Yes, please.

> *Jesus leaves.*

LAURA: *(Smiling)* From what I see, he's just like all the rest.

MARY: Worse, much worse, but I have to put up with him. At least he's honest; I think he is, anyway.

LAURA: Well, that's something.

MARY: *(Worried)* Is anyone cold? Maybe we would have been better off in the living room or the library, but it was so hot all day that I thought. . .

LAURA: You chose the best place. I don't know about everyone else, but I prefer to be a little cold to being hot.

ANDREA: I feel the same way. I prefer the cold: it sort of makes one's clothing look better.

MARY: I'm going to the kitchen to make sure he's getting the coffee hot enough.

> *Mary makes a move to leave. Laura stops her. Then Andrea will stop her. They are practically pulling at each other while they exchange the following polite words.*

LAURA: *(To Mary, holding her back)* Don't bother, dear Mary, we ate such a plentiful and delicious dinner. Why don't you just sit with us a moment longer? *(Laura makes Mary sit down.)* You must be exhausted.

MARY: *(Getting up and trying to leave. Andrea stands up and blocks her way. They make movements like football players blocking each other.)* No, no, not at all. I never get tired when I'm doing things I enjoy.

ANDREA: It's not fair that instead of our celebrating you on your birthday you're the one who's been working and working. If you'd like I can check on the coffee.

Now it's Mary's turn to block Andrea.

MARY: Thank you, darling, but that won't be necessary. Everything's ready, at least I hope it is. You know how it is with the help these days!

The three women line up as in a Greek chorus. They take on tragic looks.

LAURA: Oh me, oh my. Eulalia's been gone since Monday. I'm starting to suspect I've lost her forever.

ANDREA: Oh, me, oh, my. Petra turned out to be sassy and I have to put up with her. Yesterday she asked me for a television set for her room!

MARY: Oh, me, oh, my, oh dear me! Mercedes and Socorro have given their notice. They're going to work in a factory. They'll stay if I raise their salary one hundred percent, give them the weekends off, pay their social security, and who knows what else!

THE THREE, TOGETHER: Poor us! What will our future be without our maids!

JOSE MANUEL: *(Interrupting them. To his wife Laura)* That's enough now. We don't want to start talking about maids. *(He laughs.)*

LAURA: For us it's a subject of vital importance.

MARY: That's right. Doing without them is for us what doing without a secretary or a sales manager is for you.

TONY: As always, you're absolutely right, dear. We understand. We're the first to admit that managing a household is one of the most burdensome and least appreciated jobs that exist.

JOSE MANUEL: Let's have a round of applause for our wives' work.

> *The three women stand. The men applaud and whistle. The women accept the homage modestly.*

TONY: Fortunately, you all aren't among those women who insist on working. You have plenty of time to dedicate to our happy homes.

LAURA: And we do it with pleasure. That's why we chose to marry. I still hang on to the idea that a woman's first duty is to attend to her home.

ANDREA: I don't understand those girls who haven't even been married a year and are already looking for jobs. *(Reflecting on this:)* I can assure you they don't do it out of necessity. Absolutely not!

MARY: They do it because they're frivolous. The money they earn they throw away on fancy clothes, theater tickets, soda pop.

LAURA: Morality is on the wane. Every time I go into a bank or a government office and I see those girls. . . Well, I'd better not go on.

ANDREA: Fortunately we were educated differently, with principles.

MARY: When I got married they still read Ocampo's letter. I don't understand why they stopped. It was beautiful.

LAURA: We women have to accept the biological and social fact that men are stronger and more intelligent. *(The men take the poses of Olympic athletes.)* If that weren't true, women would have already taken over the world, since we've always outnumbered the men.

MARY: You don't know how pleased I am to hear talk like that. I see why people say you and your husband are a model couple. I agree totally. Women should be sweet and submissive *(the other two sigh)* and men strong and protective. *(They go to their wives' sides and stand like bodyguards.)* *(To Paulino:)* I'm interested in your point of view as a man. What do you think? *(His wife looks at him, begging him not to say anything stupid.)*

PAULINO: Well, I. . .

MARY: Wait, first you have to tell me what you thought of my recipe for the cod. When they told me a Spaniard was coming, I almost changed the menu out of pure fright.

PAULINO: Well. . . *(His wife takes his hand and looks at him anxiously.)* What can I say? Delicious! I haven't had better even in my country!

MARY: *(Surprised)* Really? Are you sure you liked it?

PAULINO: Very much. I told you, not even in my country, which is really saying a lot.

MARY: Thank you, thank you so much, that's the nicest compliment I've had in years.

LAURA: Don't be so modest, Mary, we all know you're an extraordinary cook.

ANDREA: Where did you learn to prepare cod? My husband is always begging for Spanish dishes and the truth is they don't come out too well when I try them. The only thing I've learned is the Spanish omelet.

MARY: I learned in Bilbao. The woman who used to clean my room gave me the recipe and then even invited me to her house to try it. Those people are very sweet.

JOSE MANUEL: They love Mexicans over there.

EVERYONE: That's true.

MARY: My experience has been that people love us everywhere we go, I don't know why, but they do. Why, even in Paris, where the people are famous for being rude, we were treated very well. *(To Tony.)* Right, dear?

TONY: That's right.

MARY: Do you remember that taxi driver who took us around and explained everything to us? He was a love. Too bad we couldn't understand him.

TONY: He charged enough.

MARY: That was his right. But his attitude is what counts. Every time I wanted to get out of the car he ran around to open the door for me. . . But we're getting off the subject. Paulino was going to give us his opinion about men and women. Spaniards have the reputation for being very domineering *(smiling)*; I read somewhere that they're all like bullfighters trying to control the bull.

PAULINO: I know of quite a few who have died from the horns. *(He laughs. No one else laughs. Andrea looks at him, irritated.)*

MARY:*(Ignoring the joke)*   What is your opinion?

PAULINO: *(Thinking hard)*   Well, that women are full of grace and all men need to do is adore them.

> *Bullfight music is heard. Paulino walks around the room as if he had cut off the ear and tail of the bull. Everyone applauds him and shout "ole."*

MARY: *(Sighing)*   How lovely!

> *Jesus enters with the tray of glasses. Tony goes to the portable bar and takes out two bottles. He begins to fill the guests' glasses. While he pours, the others chat.*

TONY:*(To Jose Manuel)*   Cognac or a creme?

JOSE MANUEL: I prefer cognac.

TONY: *(Boasting)*   Did you see what it is? *(Shows him the bottle)* It's been in my cellar for ten years. But I said to myself, what better occasion to take it out than my wife's birthday and these wonderful guests?

JOSE MANUEL: You don't see this brand anymore.

TONY: *(Secretly)* I have a full case *(joking)*, if you behave I'll give you one to take home.

JOSE MANUEL: I won't do anything naughty. *(They laugh.)*

LAURA: *(To Mary)* I thought Rosa Estela was going to be at dinner.

MARY: Don't mention her to me. She really made my blood boil today. I don't know who these young girls think they are.

LAURA: She's a teenager.

MARY: But she acts like a child.

LAURA: What did she do?

MARY: She announced she was going to Cuernavaca with some girlfriends. I told her it was my birthday and about this dinner.

Do you think she cared? Since she knows her father's always
on her side. . .

LAURA: Who'd she go with?

MARY: Some friends from school.

LAURA: Is it co-ed?

MARY: Of course it's co-ed. I'm not going to send my daughter to
one of the Catholic schools so the nuns can fill her with fear. I
want her to be free.

LAURA: Aren't you afraid?

MARY: Afraid of what?

LAURA: I don't know. She's young.

MARY: My daughter has received a perfect education. She has my
complete trust. She knows what the limits are and she'll stop
there.

TONY:(*To Andrea*) What would you like?

ANDREA: Anything would be fine.

TONY: How about an almond creme; someone brought it to me from
Italy.

ANDREA: Thank you.

TONY: (*To Paulino*) I don't have to ask you. I know you want
cognac. Am I wrong?

PAULINO: You're the boss.

MARY: Aren't you going to offer me anything? (*Smiling.*) These
husbands. Even on my birthday. . .

TONY: Sorry, dear, I was attending to our guests first. What would
you like?

MARY: Laura first.

LAURA: Nothing for me, thanks. I don't drink. (*Smiling.*) I have
other vices.

MARY: Me too, but for now I'll have to make do with a glass of
creme. (*Tony pours and distributes drinks.*)

TONY: And the coffee?

MARY: It's coming. Lukewarm coffee is not coffee.

PAULINO: The same's true of women! (*He laughs alone at his own
joke. Andrea tugs at the arms of his jacket. He stops
laughing.*)

MARY: Sorry, I don't get it.

PAULINO: Well, it's just that that's the way coffee should be drunk:
very hot.

JOSE MANUEL: Let's toast to the birthday girl.

> *They all raise their cordial glasses, except Laura, who raises her glass of mineral water. The congratulations and thank yous (by Mary) will be simultaneous.*

MARY: I accept, as long as no one asks how old I am. I've forgotten that forever. *(She laughs.)*

JOSE MANUEL: To you, on your birthday.

ANDREA: And to all your birthdays to come.

MARY: I'm not having anymore. I'm sticking with this number.

PAULINO: Congratulations.

TONY:*(Kissing his wife on the cheek)*   To the most beautiful of women. *(He takes a drink.)*

MARY: *(Drying her eyes)*   You've made me cry. Thank you, thank you all of you. *(She leans on her husband's shoulder.)*

> *They all drink. When they have finished the couples separate and form two groups, one male and one female. This movement should be natural, quotidian. The dialogues which follow should be simultaneous but   we should be able to hear what is said in both groups.*

ANDREA: *(To Mary)*   Your cod was out of this world, but tell me, where did you get the saffron? It did have saffron in it, didn't it? *(Mary nods her head "yes.")* Who sold it to you? I can't find any of that quality.

MARY: I get it from an acquaintance of my husband's, a man who imports things. He brought it to me last week and I almost told him to forget it. What prices!

ANDREA: I can imagine. A year ago it already cost an arm and a leg.

MARY: Well, now it costs twice that. It's outrageous. If it weren't from Spain I'd never have bought it.

LAURA: What's going to become of us? Before you know it we won't be able to get anything and what we do find is going to be way beyond our means.

*At the other side the men are talking,
simultaneously with the previous speeches
by the women.*

JOSE MANUEL: So when do we get started?

TONY: Soon. I spoke to Manuel today.

PAULINO: My father-in-law?

TONY: That's right. He says he's about to get the three million we
   need.

JOSE MANUEL: The parts business is the thing now. No one can
   buy new, so they buy the parts.

TONY: It's always been a good business.

JOSE MANUEL: We could have outlets all over the country.

TONY: First we have to get the ones in the city set up and running.
   Don't be in such a hurry.

JOSE MANUEL: Do you have the permits yet?

TONY: Of course, you know with a little money anything can be
   arranged. God bless Mexico!

JOSE MANUEL: That's what I say. In my line of work a small cut
   to the union delegation and all the problems disappear. It's
   better than trying to deal with the workers: what a group of
   bastards. About a month ago they threatened to strike if I didn't
   put in lunch rooms. Lunch rooms! They work little enough
   as it is. Imagine with lunch rooms inside the plant!

PAULINO: A worker's day is long and they have to eat.

JOSE MANUEL: Nobody's keeping them from eating. Let them
   bring their sandwiches and eat them wherever they want.

PAULINO: It's better if you sit at a table.

JOSE MANUEL: You're some sort of a socialist, aren't you?

PAULINO: What?

JOSE MANUEL: You chose the wrong wife. She's from a capitalist
   family.

PAULINO: I wasn't saying. . .

JOSE MANUEL: You start out giving them lunch rooms and they
   end up owners of the factories.

TONY: That's the truth. Give them an inch and they'll take a mile.
   I've never met a worker who hasn't tried to take advantage.

PAULINO: They're not all like that.

TONY: All of them! They start calling in sick to get out of working. The women get pregnant for the same reason and they all go on strike for any reason at all. Whenever I see the first worker start to act up, I don't think twice about it: I kick him right out. You have to get at the cancer when it begins.

LAURA: *(Who has been listening to the conversation of the men, interrupts)* Listen to the men! They wouldn't let us talk about maids and children and they're talking about business. It's not fair.

JOSE MANUEL: *(Bothered, but controlling himself)* OK, darling, what would you like us to talk about?

LAURA: Anything. We could talk about this last opera season. I personally thought it was wonderful.

MARY: *(Gets up from her chair. She strikes the pose of an opera diva. Very vain. The other three women do the same, in turn)* You're absolutely correct. There's no opera like the San Francisco Opera. Not long ago I saw Aida there, with a camel, elephants. . .

LAURA: *(Interrupting her. More vain. Like a diva)* The San Francisco Opera is nothing compared to the New York opera. Those are real performances: the best singers, the best set design, the best orchestras, the best directors.

ANDREA: *(Same style)* I don't agree. Neither of those operas is good. It's all show. All production. Ever since I was a girl I've been going to the Scala de Milan's season. That's opera. It's not insignificant that opera was born there. What voices! What musicality! Especially when they do Verdi. *(She sighs. Then she hums part of a Verdi opera, one of the more familiar arias.)*

MARY: No, I can't stand Verdi. He's so dull and repetitive. I'll stick with Wagner. That's real music. *(She hums something by Wagner.)*

LAURA: You'll call me a romantic, but I would kill for Puccini. *(She hums something by Puccini.)*

> *The three women, at the same time and like opera singers, hum the music they chose. They make gestures like opera singers. When they have finished, they smile and*

thank the imaginary audience for its applause.
They go to their seats.

PAULINO: I have to confess that to me the opera. . .

He shrugs his shoulders. There is a short
silence. Everyone looks discreetly at the
person next to him. Laura lifts a finger to
her nose and pretends to scratch it. Paulino
reacts and continues talking.

PAULINO: I just go to please her. *(He caresses his wife.)* The truth
is I'm happier at the musical revues in Madrid.

ANDREA: How can you even compare. . .

LAURA: Do you mean those shows where the women come out
wearing capes? When I was little my parents took me to see
one, The Eve of the Foot Washing I think it was called.

PAULINO: *(Indignant)* The Eve of the Dove, if you will, the revue
of all revues.

LAURA: No, that's not what it was called. I remember the title was
sort of funny.

PAULINO: Well it's better than those traviatas with tuberculosis or
those butterflies that commit harikari because a sad gringo
sailor stood her up.

LAURA: She had a daughter. By the American.

PAULINO: Why didn't she have it by a Japanese! No, she had to get
involved with a gringo, the one with the dollars.

LAURA: That was her choice.

PAULINO: What do you mean "choice." It was that damned
propaganda. We have to consume American products even if
they poison us.

JOSE MANUEL: And are the Russian products any better?

PAULINO: I don't know, since they don't allow us to get them here.

JOSE MANUEL: They're junk. Anyway, they're scarce.

PAULINO: How do you know?

There is another silence. Now the looks are
more inquisitive, but everyone rectifies them

instantly. Laura holds her nose and then scratches it.

PAULINO: Whew! It smells like gas! *(His wife tugs at his jacket more forcefully than before.)* But, dear. . . *(She tugs at his jacket. He shuts up.)*

MARY: Do you smell gas? That's strange. *(She sniffs.)* Well, yes, I guess it does smell a bit. If you'll excuse me, I'll just check in the kitchen to see if the stove is turned off. You can never be too sure. *(She leaves quickly.)*

ANDREA: *(With a forced smile)* I've always said gas is dangerous. You saw that pipe that exploded the other day. . . I don't know how many people were hurt. I'm terrified of gas. That's why I only use my microwave oven. It's marvelous. In five minutes your dinner is ready. I can't believe how much time I've saved since they brought it to me from the States.

TONY: *(Poking fun)* Did your husband bring it to you? The man who doesn't like American products?

PAULINO: Her father brought it.

LAURA: I foolishly bought one here. The next week it broke down, just like everything they say we make so well.

ANDREA: I can assure you yours cost more than mine. Everything is better made there and cheaper, not to mention the service and the warranties. There's no comparison, there the warranties are real and they're good for twenty years. And the quality. *(She goes to Laura and shows her dress.)* Guess how much this dress cost me in Houston?

LAURA: *(Bothered by Andrea's conceitedness)* I don't know, it's so lovely.

ANDREA: Name a price, any price.

LAURA: I don't dare.

ANDREA: It only cost me six hundred dollars, a steal! When would you find anything like this here for that price? *(She fingers the cloth of her dress.)* Feel this fabric.

LAURA: *(Touching the fabric)* Wonderful! *(Conceited.)* It's as pretty as the dresses they sell in Paris. *(Modestly, she indicates her dress.)* Like this one.

ANDREA: *(Smiling falsely)* Is it a Dior?

LAURA: No, it's a Belanciaga, I like them better. Dior is a little out of style now.
ANDREA: *(Hypocritical)* It's divine!
PAULINO: Can I touch the fabric?
ANDREA: You're not touching anything, do you hear?
PAULINO: I just wanted to compare.

> *Mary returns.*

MARY: Don't worry. Lupe had let one of the pilot lights on the stove go out, but it's all fixed now.
JOSE MANUEL: How careless!
MARY: I know it, but what can you do? You can't even scold one since right away they announce they're leaving. *(Changing the topic.)* What were you talking about while I was in the kitchen?
LAURA: Nothing. Clothes. We were just commenting that in Mexico you can never get the same quality as abroad or in the States, although I do admit that if you look hard you can find some cute stuff, you know, for everyday wear.
MARY: I never buy anything here. It doesn't fit. The same is true for Parisian clothes. I get the best fit in Amsterdam.
PAULINO: The Dutch women are a little heavier.
MARY: I beg your pardon!
PAULINO: *(His wife is pulling at his jacket)* Nothing, nothing.
LAURA: Andrea's dress is from Houston.
ANDREA: And Laura's is from Paris.

> *The three women act out a fashion show.*
> *Each one will model in front of the men,*
> *who applaud. The scene will be silent,*
> *accompanied by appropriate music. The*
> *women act out a second round. This time*
> *they are more sensual and vulgar. They*
> *begin a strip tease which they will not finish.*
> *The men will react in a macho, vulgar way.*
> *They will try to pinch the women or pat*
> *them on the bottom. When the fashion show*
> *is finished, the women straighten their*

> *clothing and everyone becomes respectable
> again.*

TONY: Would anyone like another drink? If you don't like what's in the bar, just tell me what you want. That's what my cellar is for.

PAULINO: Well, I would prefer a brandy, Spanish, if you have it.

TONY: Perfect. How about you, Jose Manuel?

JOSE MANUEL: Cognac, please.

TONY: And for the ladies?

ANDREA: I prefer to wait for the coffee.

MARY: Where's my head!! I forgot the coffee. *(She gets up and goes to the door.)*

ANDREA: That's all right. Don't bother. I'm fine.

MARY: He should have brought it out already. *(Shouting off stage.)* Jesus! Jesus!

> *Jesus enters.*

JESUS: Yes, ma'am?

MARY: What happened to the coffee?

JESUS: I was waiting for you to tell me to bring it out.

MARY: *(Shaking her head)* Bring it out immediately!

JESUS: Yes, ma'am.

MARY: You have to be on top of them all the time. *(She goes to her seat. To Andrea)* It won't be long.

ANDREA: Thank you.

> *Again there is total silence. Someone coughs. Laura discreetly takes out her hanky and pretends to blow her nose. Everyone looks at each other furtively.*

PAULINO: *(To Andrea, in a low voice)* Someone's about to shit his pants, for Christ's sake!

ANDREA: *(Low voice)* Please, Paulino.

LAURA: *(In a low voice, to her husband)* What manners! I'll bet it's the Spaniard.

JOSE MANUEL: I don't think so. I'd bet on the lady of the house. See how fat she is, and how much she ate?

MARY: *(To Tony)* You didn't do that, did you?

TONY: How can you say that?

> *Mary gets up nervously, goes to a bureau,*
> *brings a candelabrum puts it on the coffee*
> *table, asks for a match, gives it to Jose*
> *Manuel, lights the candles. She smiles.*

MARY: They say a lighted candle is good for getting rid of . . . *(Short pause)* the smell of cigarettes.

PAULINO: Nobody's been smoking. *(His wife pulls at his jacket.)*

TONY: *(Reacting)* Would anyone like a cigar? Someone brought them to me from Havana. It's the only good thing left on the poor island.

MARY: No, God no! Do you want us women to get sick? If the gentlemen wish to smoke cigars, they'll have to go to the library or to the living room; and that way we could have a chance to talk about our children and our maids. *(They all laugh.)*

ANDREA: *(To Laura)* Have you gone to the theater lately?

LAURA: Yes, I went to the Fabregas last week. A terrific play, I really recommend it.

ANDREA: What's it called?

LAURA: I can't remember, something about love in, or love under, or love on. . .

PAULINO:*(Laughing)* It's not the same: love on or under or in. *(He laughs alone. They all look at him accusingly. He gets serious.)*

LAURA: *(As if she hadn't been interrupted)* But the title's not important. Everything they do there is good.

ANDREA: I on the other hand had to go to a high school play. Enriqueta invited me, I don't know if you remember her, the teacher. What a disaster! They did something called The Workers. You should have heard the language, and you know I don't get put off by much. I consider myself to be a modern, liberated woman. But that was something else. . .

LAURA: Did you walk out?

ANDREA: I couldn't, I would have had to walk right across the stage, so I had to sit through the whole thing. Naturally there was a sex scene.

LAURA: A Mexican author?

ANDREA: Of course.

LAURA: I knew it. I don't understand why they don't choose something decent to put on in the schools. There are plenty of good plays out there.

ANDREA: It's because of the lack of values, not just in the theater: everywhere.

PAULINO: I liked it.

ANDREA: How can you say you liked it? That day you said it was vulgar.

PAULINO: That's what you said.

ANDREA: I said it but you didn't contradict me.

PAULINO: You didn't let me speak.

ANDREA: *(Getting angry)* So, I don't let you speak?

PAULINO: Well, you talk like all women.

JOSE MANUEL: *(Laughing)* That is, a lot.

TONY: *(Laughing)* They're like waterfalls with words flowing in every direction.

> *A choreography begins. The three women stand in one corner of an imaginary boxing ring, the three men in another. They all begin to do warm-up exercises. At one point one turns into a manager and towels the other or maybe is the announcer of the fight. The all take part in the fight. When the bell rings, Jesus enters with the coffee service.*

PAULINO: *(Announcing at the center of the ring)* In this corner, Mary, a heavyweight! Here we have Laura, a featherweight, and Andrea, a bantamweight. *(He goes to his corner. Now Mary will announce:)*

MARY: And in the other corner, all heavyweights: Tony, Jose Manuel and Paulino.

*They all jump into the ring. They greet the
audience. The bell for the first round rings.
Jesus enters with the coffee tray.*

JESUS: Here's the coffee, ma'am. *(No one pays any attention. The
boxers make boxing movements: they punch each other, dance
around, etc.)*

> *As they converse, they will continue with the
> boxing movements. Jesus sits with the
> imaginary audience. Logically, he cheers for
> the men. He will shout when he thinks they
> are going to win or when they utter biting
> phrases.*

MARY: Deep down all men want to be women. They are jealous of
our ability to bear children.
PAULINO: Yeah, yeah, I'm dying of envy. *(He laughs loudly.)*
ANDREA: Feminine superiority begins at an early age. When we
become women they are still children.
TONY: Admit we're superior. God's a man.
LAURA: And the Virgin a woman. She was His mother. How do
you like that? If she hadn't wanted, no God.
PAULINO: What about the geniuses. Name me a woman musician
that reaches Beethoven's feet or a woman writer like
Shakespeare. Go ahead, go ahead.
ANDREA: Women haven't reached genius status because men have
had them enslaved. But all that's about to change.
TONY: Poor little slaves. So abandoned. Never able to defend
themselves.
ANDREA: Machos!
PAULINO: Cows!
MARY: Conceited bastards!
TONY: Stupid bitches!
MARY: Useless wimps!
JOSE MANUEL: Kept women!

> *The bell rings. Everyone freezes for an
> instant. Jesus, who had been gesticulating
> and shouting, straightens his jacket and offers
> coffee again.*

MARY: I don't think there's any point in discussing if the male sex or the female sex is superior. I think we have gone beyond such discussions.

JOSE MANUEL: Naturally. I don't think that in this day and age anyone still thinks he's superior to anyone else. Not with regard to sex nor race nor color.

MARY: Well, I wouldn't go that far. Let's just leave it at sex.

JESUS: May I serve the coffee now?

MARY: In just a minute. I'll call you.

JESUS: As you wish, ma'am.

MARY: I'm sure he came in just to hear what we were saying. He's the best example of why we still can't talk about the equality of races. There's no way around it: they're inferior.

> *Another silence. Laura, this time making no attempt at discretion, takes out her handkerchief and holds her nose. Paulino elbows his wife and laughs loudly. Andrea blushes. Everyone turns slightly toward Jose Manuel. When Laura realizes this she gets up and goes to the other side of the terrace and starts to cry. Jose Manuel follows her.*

JOSE MANUEL: What's the matter? Do you feel ill? *(Laura cries harder.)*

MARY: *(Hurrying to Laura's side)* What's the matter with your wife? She's not sick, is she?

JOSE MANUEL: I don't know.

MARY: *(To Laura)* Let's see, now, what's the matter, are we feeling poorly?

LAURA: It's nothing, thank you. *(She sobs.)*

MARY: It must be something. A person doesn't cry like that for no reason. Trust me, I'm your friend. You know all of us here are fond of you.

LAURA: *(Crying out)* I'm leaving. I can't stay in a place where this buffoon *(points to her husband)* is trying to make a fool out of me.

> *Laura goes to the other limit of the terrace, followed by her husband.*

JOSE MANUEL: But, Laura, dear, I. . .

LAURA: Don't Laura me! If you absolutely had to give way to all that farting you could have at least excused yourself and gone to the bathroom. You're a disgusting pig!

JOSE MANUEL: *(Bothered)* I haven't been farting. You can bet it was one of your friends. *(He points to the others.)* Your friends, not mine.

LAURA: *(Tight-lipped, furious)* They're my father's business partners, and they're going to be yours.

JOSE MANUEL: I don't give a damn who they are. My friends, for your information, belong to a totally different class.

LAURA: Yes, I know, Arturo and the others, right? Those are your friends. Drunks, all of them!

JOSE MANUEL: *(Raising his voice)* I won't allow you to. . .

LAURA: You don't do the allowing, do you hear me? Not the slightest bit.

PAULINO: *(To his wife)* Good God! They're fighting big time, and all over a little fart that guy let. *(He points to Tony.)*

ANDREA: Paulino, please!

PAULINO: What do you expect to happen after we're served cod bought in any crummy grocery store. Did you notice she didn't even put capers on it?

ANDREA: Shut up!

PAULINO: *(Bothered)* Nobody tells me to shut up. God damn it. I'll shit on the Virgin!

TONY: *(Who heard this last remark)* Sir, I can't permit you to say such things. You have no right to bring our Mother Church into this! *(He crosses himself.)*

PAULINO: I'm free to say whatever I damned well please. That's why I have these balls you know. Christ!

TONY: *(Standing face-to-face with Paulino)* Well you'll have to go fuck your mother. In this home we respect the church before all else and no God-damned Spic is going to come along to make asinine remarks.

PAULINO: Shit-eating church-goer!

> *The two men stand face to face, gesticulating. They reach the point of grabbing each other's shirts and pushing, but go no further. Mary indignantly pulls Tony away and makes him face her.*

MARY: Didn't I tell you? What a nice way to celebrate my birthday. Instead of inviting my family and my friends you had to bring these. . . *(Brief pause)*, these. . . Even on my birthday you can only think about business!

TONY: *(Laughing sarcastically)* Your family? You wanted me to invite your family over to finish off all my wines! Ha!

> *The following dialogues will be simultaneous but at least the gist of each one should be understood.*

LAURA: *(To Jose Manuel)* As far as I'm concerned you can begin divorce proceedings tomorrow. If you don't I will; I'm sick and tired of you and your vulgarity, do you hear me? Sick and tired of it!

JOSE MANUEL: And I'm tired of your stupidity, you diaper-soiling child!

PAULINO: *(To Andrea)* Who does he think he is *(pointing to Tony)*, that shit-eating rich man. And he'd better not get my dander up, 'cause I'm capable of airing his dirty laundry. As if I didn't know where his money comes from.

ANDREA: Let it go, please.

PAULINO: Nobody insults me. Yes I am a Spic, and proud of it; I'm honorable and hard-working, not hypocritical like them.

MARY: *(To Tony)* I forbid you to insult my family, you, of all people, with those relatives I won't even mention!

TONY: Say it, let's see if you dare. At least they're not perpetual loafers like yours. Don't forget that if I hadn't taken you out of that atmosphere right now you'd be a miserable secretary, if that.

MARY: And if it hadn't been for me you'd have married a bitch just like your mother.

TONY: You idiot!

MARY: You jerk!

TONY: You lame brain!

MARY: *(Shouting even louder)* Asshole!

JESUS: *(Hurrying to Mary's side)* You called?

MARY: No, I didn't. I was talking to a different asshole. Get out of here!

JESUS: Yes, ma'am. *(He leaves hurriedly.)*

ANDREA: *(Very nervous)* I'm not feeling well, I'm leaving.

She takes her purse, walks, drops the purse, bends to pick it up as the men hurry to do the same. As she is bending over, Andrea emits a loud fart. She and the men who are also bending over freeze for an instant. The men straighten up and pretend they haven't seen or heard anything.

ANDREA: *(Quietly, embarrassed)* Excuse me.

Everyone looks at her. They don't know how to react until Jose Manuel takes the lead, defending her.

JOSE MANUEL: I'm the one who should excuse himself. I'm the one who. . . *(Brief pause)* passed gas.

TONY: *(Not to be outdone)* No, no, it was me. I'm the owner of the house *(points to Andrea)* and that gas was mine.

PAULINO: Fuck! You've got no reason to be excusing yourself. I was the one who accidentally let one slip.

MARY: It's OK, all of you. This could happen to anyone, it's quite natural.

JOSE MANUEL: Of course it's natural. See how easy it is for a little wind to escape?

Jose Manuel half sits in the air and pushes. Nothing comes out.

PAULINO: Not like that, man. Like this. *(He also half sits and pushes. He gets red in the face and hits his stomach to try to move the gases around.)* Christ, it won't come out!

MARY: That's enough, for God's sake. Even I felt a little while ago a petite flatulence trying to escape, but I held it back. If you want, I can give it a try. *(She bends down and pushes.)*

LAURA: Don't bother on our account.

MARY: It's no bother, really. *(She pushes again.)*

TONY: See? Nothing's happened here at all. *(To Mary)* What about the coffee you promised us? *(To the others.)* I beg you to return to your seats.

*They all get comfortable in their seats. Mary
turns toward the door.*

MARY: Jesus, Jesus!

JESUS: *(Entering)* At your service, ma'am.

MARY: What are you waiting for to bring the coffee out?

JESUS: You said. . .

MARY: Bring it out this instant!

JESUS: Yes, ma'am. *(He leaves.)*

MARY: *(Trying to break the tension)* My, but we're serious! Today
is my birthday and I want everyone to be happy. What if we
dance a little?

LAURA: What a marvelous idea. That will help our dinner set.

PAULINO: Put on something lively, like a paso doble or a choti.

MARY: *(Smiling)* I'm afraid I don't have that kind of music.

TONY: I'm going to play some romantic music for you. I have a Ray
Conniff record you'll just love.

JOSE MANUEL: Why not a mambo or a cha-cha-cha? Something
to create atmosphere.

TONY: *(Laughing)* You mean an outdated atmosphere. People now
dance to hard rock.

JOSE MANUEL: The mambo's much better. Have you got any
cumbia? *(He sings and dances a few steps from "La pollera
colora.")*

TONY: *(Laughing)* I for one am not up for those rhythms, so I'll put
on "Strangers in the Night" by Bert Kemfer. What do you say?

PAULINO: Put on whatever you want. I'm not going to dance
anyway.

MARY: In my house everyone dances, I don't want to hear that you
don't want to.

TONY: Excuse me, I'll just go into the other room where my set is. I
only have the speakers in here. *(He points to the speakers, then
leaves.)*

MARY:*(Smiling):* He's afraid that if I touch his stereo set I'll wreck it.
He guards it more carefully than he does his daughter, the light
of his life.

JOSE MANUEL: He's got a nice set.

LAURA: Apparently all men are alike. Jose Manuel takes better care
of his set than he does of me. And he won't let me touch it
either. They must think we have steel hands or I don't know
what.

JOSE MANUEL: *(Smiling)* Stop exaggerating.

> *"Strangers in the Night" is heard at top
> volume. Tony returns.*

MARY: *(Shouting)* Tony dear, please lower the volume a little. We're not deaf.
TONY: It's not very loud.
MARY: I don't want to have to shout.
TONY: *(Shrugging)* I'll go turn it down. *(He leaves.)*
MARY: He always has to turn it all the way up. I don't know what pleasure it brings him.
LAURA: *(Also shouting)* That's the style, now, it's the same in the discotheques.
MARY: I never go to those places. What nightmares!
ANDREA: I like them.
MARY: Well, of course, you're young.

> *The volume of the music goes down. Now
> it's almost imperceptible. Tony enters. He
> smiles.*

TONY: How's that?
MARY: Men, men! They always have to exaggerate. That's why there'll always be wars. *(To Tony)* Love, now we can hardly hear it. We can't dance with it like that.
TONY: You said. . .
MARY: Forget it, I'll go.

> *She starts to leave. Tony runs past her and
> leaves.*

TONY: No, no, I'll go.

> *Mary smiles. She returns to the others.*

MARY: I assure you that now he'll put it at normal volume.

> *The music is now heard at a normal volume.
> Mary smiles triumphantly. Her husband
> enters. The two of them smile.*

TONY: Now, let's dance, everyone.

> *Tony takes his wife's hand and starts to dance. Likewise, Laura and Jose Manuel. Paulino remains seated. Mary interrupts the dance and goes toward Paulino and Andrea, pulling her husband by the hand.*

MARY: Aren't you going to ask your wife to dance?
PAULINO: I don't know how to dance.
MARY: I don't believe you. Dance with me.
PAULINO: It's true.
MARY: Come here.

> *She pulls away from her husband and grabs Paulino. She rubs against him and dances cheek-to-cheek with him. Tony asks Andrea to dance. Andrea watches her husband the whole time. Jealous, she stops dancing, goes to her husband, pulls at him.*

ANDREA: *(To Mary)* Excuse me. I wouldn't want my husband to step on you.
MARY: Nonsense! He's a good dancer.
ANDREA: I'll return your husband to you.

> *Tony dances with his wife. All three couples dance the whole song. When it ends, Paulino tries to sit down. His wife stops him. Another song from the same record begins to play. Everyone dances wildly, even Paulino, who does so somewhat stiffly. Then they all stop dancing at the same time. Without trying to cover up their actions, they all hold their noses.*

LAURA: The odor is coming from that direction. *(She points to Andrea.)* Not again! Careful, dear, sometimes those little gusts of wind come accompanied! You wouldn't want to soil your darling 600 dollar dress bought at the flea market, would you? *(She laughs.)*
ANDREA: *(Furious)* We can all see that that's where you do your shopping. What taste!

LAURA: As if you had any! Just look at that husband of yours!
PAULINO: *(Offended)* Ugly but virile, ask her. *(He points to his wife.)* Whereas I'll bet these guys can't even get it up.
JOSE MANUEL: Loan me your old lady and I'll show her what's supposed to go on in bed.
MARY: *(To Tony)* What are you waiting for? Get these hicks out of my house! I can't take any more!
TONY: They're not going anywhere. They're my friends and my business partners and you might as well hear the truth: they're all worth more than you!

Enter Jesus with the coffee tray.

MARY: *(The sight of Jesus makes her furious)* Get out of here! *(Jesus runs out. Off stage we hear the noise of cups and plates breaking.)* That's all I need! My Bavarian tea service!
ANDREA: *(Fanning herself with her hand)* Mother of God, I'm fainting!

Andrea falls slowly to the floor. They all run to help her. Jose Manuel and Tony lift her up and, almost dragging her, take her to a sofa that is a little farther away than the ones in the center of the terrace.

PAULINO: Leave my wife alone! She's not a sack of potatoes. Shit! *(He goes to his wife and fusses over her. The others stand back a bit.)* You'd take any opportunity to feel a woman up. *(To Andrea, brusquely.)* Are you feeling better?
MARY: What's the matter with her? Did the food disagree with her?
PAULINO: Nothing, you fuckers! Can't you tell when a woman's pregnant?
MARY: Pregnant? Oh, yes, of course, pregnant, oh, that's wonderful! *(To the others)* Did you hear? Andrea's expecting a baby! *(To Paulino and Andrea)* Congratulations. I mean it, congratulations. Motherhood is the best thing that can happen to a woman. *(To the others)* Don't you agree?

Everyone gets up, including Andrea. They recite as if from memory:

LAURA: Motherhood is sublime.

JOSE MANUEL: Motherhood transforms a woman into an artist and even into God. It's creative!

PAULINO: The only valid role for a woman is that of mother.

ANDREA: The world will continue to exist as long as women continue to bear children.

TONY: I recognize woman's superiority to man. She bears the children.

ALL: Motherhood is the most.

> *They all return to their seats. They become*
> *natural again.*

LAURA: How exciting! I hope you'll have twins!

PAULINO: One's enough.

LAURA: *(Conceited again)* This reminds me of my last pregnancy. I was so sick! I thought I would die. If it weren't for Dr. Fernandez, who's become quite famous since then, I wouldn't be telling this.

ANDREA: *(Trying to get up. To her husband)* Paulino, get me out of here. It stinks worse over here.

> *Mary approaches the sofa where Andrea is*
> *resting. She sniffs around. Paulino goes to*
> *her side.*

MARY: It's true. Whew!

> *Paulino helps Andrea move, Mary continues*
> *to sniff, now on either side of the sofa and*
> *behind it. Suddenly she breaks out laughing.*

MARY: *(Laughing)* God! *(She laughs again.)*

TONY: *(Surprised)* What are you laughing about?

MARY: Now I know who the culprit is. It's Sade!

ALL: Sade?

MARY: Yes, the dog. *(She points under the sofa.)* There he is, sleeping away and farting his brains out.

LAURA: A dog! That's a riot. *(She laughs. To her husband, in a low voice.)* Do you believe her?

JOSE MANUEL: *(Low voice)* Act like you do. *(He smiles hypocritically so no one will realize he spoke.)*

PAULINO: Jesus Christ! Who would have guessed? Just a shitty dog. *(In a low voice to his wife.)* I still think it's the old lady.
ANDREA: Please.
LAURA: And I tried to blame my husband. *(She hugs her husband.)*
JOSE MANUEL: There you have it.

> *Andrea gets up, covers her mouth with her hands and runs out.*

PAULINO: Are you going to start that vomiting again?
MARY: *(Smiling)* Pregnancy does have its little inconveniences. *(She goes to the door.)* Jesus! Jesus!
JESUS: *(Entering)* Yes, ma'am?
MARY: You may bring in the coffee now.
TONY: But first please get this furry beast out of here *(he points at the place where the dog is hiding)*, open the window and bring out the liqueurs.
JESUS: Yes, sir.
MARY: The coffee first.
JESUS: But he said. . .
MARY: The coffee first! *(She goes to Jesus and says in a low voice:)* And don't think I didn't realize you broke my tea service. It was German. We'll settle accounts later.
JESUS: Excuse me, ma'am.
MARY: Move!
JESUS: Yes, ma'am.
TONY: Don't forget the dog.

> *Jesus goes to get the dog. He pulls him out. The guests caress him when he passes by them.*

LAURA: *(Rubbing the dog's head)* You're a little stinker!
TONY: Now that the gas problem has been solved *(everyone smiles and looks at his or her neighbor suspiciously)* we can return to our places to toast to the new parents and to my wife.
LAURA: I'm not toasting until I get my coffee. I've been waiting for hours. *(She laughs.)*
MARY: I'm sorry. It's the help. They're worthless.
LAURA: I was just kidding. Don't pay any attention to me.

> *Andrea returns.*

MARY: Are you OK now?

ANDREA: Yes, thank you. Do you think I could have a cup of tea?

MARY: Of course. *(She goes to the door again.)* Jesus, Jesus! *(She waits a moment and when she sees that Jesus doesn't come, she calls again.)* Jesus!

LAURA: I don't know why you put up with that fellow. I would have fired him. On my word!

JOSE MANUEL: They're all worthless.

MARY: And thieves to boot.

PAULINO: What those guys need is to have their balls cut off. All they think about is sex. That's why they're so lazy.

> *Everyone laughs. They squeeze together in a tight circle. They talk about the dog and servants at an accelerated speed. We cannot make out what they are saying. Jesus enters. He's no longer wearing a uniform. Now he is wearing blue jeans and a plaid shirt. Everyone shuts up when they see him. Jesus approaches. He looks at them a second. He makes a raspberry sound with his mouth, which sounds like a loud fart. He laughs and exits. The others respond "Ah" to his raspberry and remain frozen.*

THE END

DATE DUE

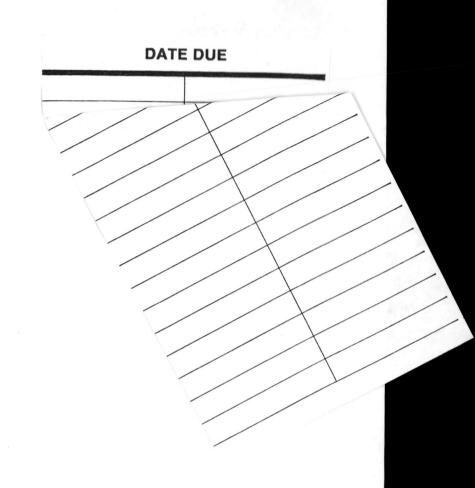

ISBN 0-9643288-0-1